KEEPING
KOI

NANCY COOPER WISNER
&
FREDERICK ALBERT SIMON

Sterling Publishing Co., Inc. New York

title page photo:
Ginrin Showa

Designed by David Levy

Library of Congress Cataloging-in-Publication Data

Wisner, Nancy Cooper.
    Keeping Koi / Nancy Cooper Wisner & Frederick Albert Simon.
       p.   cm.
    Includes index.
    ISBN 0-8069-3882-X
    1. Koi. I. Simon, Frederick Albert. II. title.
SF458.K64W57 1996
639.3′752—dc20   96-13596
                                           CIP

10 9 8 7 6 5 4 3 2 1

Published by Sterling Publishing Company, Inc.
387 Park Avenue South, New York, N.Y. 10016
© 1996 by Nancy Cooper Wisner and Frederick Albert Simon
Distributed in Canada by Sterling Publishing
℅ Canadian Manda Group, One Atlantic Avenue, Suite 105
Toronto, Ontario, Canada M6K 3E7
Distributed in Great Britain and Europe by Cassell PLC
Wellington House, 125 Strand, London WC2R 0BB, England
Distributed in Australia by Capricorn Link (Australia) Pty Ltd.
P.O. Box 6651, Baulkham Hills, Business Centre, NSW 2153, Australia
Printed and bound in China

Sterling ISBN 0-8069-3882-X

ACKNOWLEDGMENTS

Our first thank-you goes to our wonderful friend Tung Phan.
We learned a great deal about Koi from Tung and from visiting his Koi farm,
but, most important, we became lasting friends.

A special thank-you to our dear friend Bill Hackett for introducing
us to Sterling Publishing Company.

Our thanks to Koi U.S.A. *magazine and* The Magazine of the Mid-Atlantic Koi
Club, *for providing us with so many lovely Koi photographs.*

Our thanks also to Dr. Tsai Mao Lin, who provided the Taiwan pictures.

Additional pond and Koi photographs courtesy of Mid-Atlantic Koi Club members
Lew and Mary Waldeck, Donna Marie and Nick Saites,
Tom and Diana Burton, Brian Glaser, and William West.

Illustrations by James Malaro.

Photographers David Hester, Mark Milligan, Wayne Orchard,
Nuriel Guedalia, and Ray Abell.

KOHAKU

A Pond in Virginia

CONTENTS

GINRIN KOHAKU

Fish have always been a part of my life. The usual childhood goldfish that died, and black mollies given to me when I was in the eighth grade by my first boyfriend, led to an ongoing interest in tropical fish. That is, until 1971, when I moved into a log cabin in Medford Lakes, New Jersey. In the process of cleaning up the property, which was overgrown from years of neglect, I discovered a small cement pond. My son, Tom, and I worked long and hard digging out the dirt and debris until we finally had a small but very pretty pond. We added four comets and left them to their own devices.

That little cement pond sparked my interest, and a larger pond with clear water and beautiful Koi became my goal. Finally, in 1988, after a series of three ponds in the same spot (making the pond larger each time), buying Koi of inferior quality at high prices, and then killing them due to our lack of knowledge and due to bio-filters that did not perform as promised, Fred and I decided to search out the answers to successful Koi keeping.

Finding the answers was a much more difficult task than we anticipated. Information in books was confusing and contradictory. Retailers selling garden pond products and Koi either gave no information or advised incorrectly. In general, they were more interested in selling than informing. Our pond was still pea green and our Koi were not very attractive. Then we were fortunate enough to discover the Mid-Atlantic Koi Club and its members. After that, we traveled every weekend to meet with fellow Koi keepers. We learned from their experiences, good and bad, and in return shared ours with them. The Associated Koi Clubs of America gave us the opportunity to talk with and attend lectures given by Koi keepers from all over the world. The result is this book, the book I wanted 15 years ago when I started in the Koi-keeping hobby.

We hope this is the book you have been looking for, and we look forward to showing you how to become a successful Koi keeper.

NANCY COOPER WISNER
FREDERICK ALBERT SIMON

CHAPTER ONE

ALL ABOUT KOI

SHOWA

Koi are members of the carp family. They are certainly the most colorful members of the family, which is why they are often referred to as living jewels. Koi can have many colors and patterns: for example, solid colors of red, white, yellow, black, or orange, or combinations of colors, such as red and white, red and black, black and white, yellow and black, even blue and red, and more; some Koi have metallic silver and/or gold scales; some have no scales at all. The most recent variation is the butterfly (longfin) Koi. All the color combinations and scale types are defined in this book.

Koi tend to mature to a length of about 20 to 22 inches (50 to 56 cm). Larger Koi, of 30 inches (75 cm) or more, are not as common but are not rare. Koi that have grown as large as 36 inches (90 cm) and weigh 45 pounds (20 k) are more rare and highly treasured.

Koi are very social fish and happiest when schooling with other Koi. After years of collecting tropical fish and constantly having to consider which varieties were aggressive and territorial and which were not, we have found Koi a pleasure. Koi are so lacking in aggression, neither the male nor female defends their eggs after spawning. We have small Koi and large Koi living very peacefully in our pond.

The general term for Koi is *nishikigoi*, meaning brocade carp, after the beautiful Japanese brocade robes. We were taught to pronounce it "knee-she-key-goi" (as in "boy") although some pronounce it *nish'-key-goi*. We asked a Japanese gentleman who is a Koi judge, and he advised us that either is acceptable. Koi varieties, terms, and pronunciation are discussed later in this book.

The size of a Koi's environment has nothing to do with the ultimate size the Koi grows to be. A smaller or larger pond does not guarantee smaller or larger Koi. We once received a call from a woman who had two Koi in a 50 gallon (190 l) aquarium that were given to her as a gift when the Koi were very small. They had grown so large, they were no longer able to turn around in the tank. She asked if we could find a home for them, which we did. They are now living a much better life in a lovely garden pond. Just as with humans, the size of a Koi is determined by its genes; a healthy environment and good nutrition help it reach its full potential. The rate of growth depends on diet, water temperature, and water quality. You will be reading a great deal about water quality.

With good water quality and proper nutrition, you can expect your Koi to live 50 to 70 years. The record life span is held by a 226-year-old female Koi. She was cared for by generations of the same Japanese family. Traditionally, in Japan, Koi are passed down through the family. As the hobby of keeping Koi grows, this tradition could well be practiced all over the world.

The history of Koi begins in Persia. It is recorded that 2,500 years ago a son was born to Confucius. To honor the birth, King Shoko of Persia presented Confucius with a magoy. Magoy are the black carp from which all colored Koi are descended. The Chinese raised these black carp in their rice paddies as a food supplement and passed the practice on to the rice farmers in Japan. In the Niigata Prefecture of Japan, the heavy snowfall during the winter made it impossible to gather rice or net fish for food. To solve this problem, the Niigata farmers began to build ponds near their homes so

Sanke

they would have an accessible supply of fresh food throughout the winter months. The story goes that as they netted the Koi they began to notice mutants with one or more scales of different colors. These Koi were kept as pets and selectively bred. The offspring of these mutant parents were watched carefully as they developed for possible future breeding. Colored carp quickly became very popular and a new industry was born for the peasant farmers of Japan.

A drought in the latter part of the 18th century would have completely destroyed all the Koi if a few farmers had not made the wise decision to move their fish to a pond in Ojiya City. At this time in history, the breeders had been able to develop red, light yellow, and tortoiseshell Koi. It was not until 1830 that a red Koi and a white Koi were crossbred and the first *kohaku* appeared on the Koi scene. *Asagi* (blue scaled), *ki utsuri* (yellow and black) were developed in the 1880's. The selective breed-

ing process continued. During the 1930's, mirror carp, which have only a few large scales, and leather carp, which have none at all, were sent from Germany to Japan and crossed with Koi. The result of this crossbreeding was the *doitsu*.

War almost caused the annihilation of these beautiful fish. Koi were sacrificed so people could be fed. The fear among the breeders and collectors was that with so few Koi left, it would be impossible to develop again the varieties that had taken centuries of hard work and research to create. There is a happy ending to this story. Farmers in the Niigata Prefecture had protected and cared for adult Koi and the practice of breeding Koi began to thrive again.

Koi keepers all over the world take great pride in their Koi. Many enter their best in Koi shows locally and at great distances. Koi shows are held all over the world. The first was held in Japan in 1968. Most are sponsored and organized by Koi clubs and organizations. Great care is given to water

Mid-Atlantic Koi Club Show 1995,
Longwood Gardens, Kennet Square, Pa.

quality and surrounding conditions to keep these valued Koi healthy and stress-free. Shows are usually held at the end of the growing season when the Koi are at their very best in color and size.

Interestingly enough, male and female Koi are equal in beauty. Because of the size and girth of female Koi, they are often preferred by the judges. Brightness of color, conformation, balance, and a sharp, clean edge to the pattern *(kiwa)*, are all judged very closely. When a Koi has many outstanding qualities, judges will forgive a fault.

As a Koi grows and matures, its color and pattern will change, often dramatically. The Japanese have a saying, "Only a fool would buy a three-inch Koi and only a fool would sell one." A kohaku (red and white) with beautiful bright *hi* (red) as a young fish may turn pale and more orange as the Koi matures. Conversely, a muddy-looking

Ki-Ogon Butterfly (longfin) Koi

young Koi may develop into a champion with bright, clear colors and pattern. A mature Koi that has maintained its color and pattern is highly prized. Because of their friendly and trusting nature, Koi can be trained with very little effort to eat out of your hand or even come up for a kiss.

Here's how to do it: Feed the Koi at the same time every day. Put food in your hand, close your fist, pat the water, and put your hand in the pond. Release a little food at a time. Each time, let the Koi come closer to you until they take the food from your hand before you release it into the pond. Koi do not have teeth, so there is no need to fear an injury. Feeding your Koi is just one of the many pleasures of a Koi pond.

What could be more relaxing than watching your own beautiful Koi swimming peacefully in your garden pond?

Our friend Donna Marie Saites and her Koi Romeo

CHAPTER TWO

MAINTAINING HEALTHY KOI

GOROMO

Koi, like all living creatures, need a healthy environment and good nutrition to grow and develop properly. It is widely accepted that Koi carry disease and parasites all the time; however, it is only when Koi are stressed and weakened that this can become a problem. A stressed Koi may lose its slime coat, which is its protection against external parasites, fungus, and other pathogens. Providing good water, and a nutritious diet will result in stress-free, healthy Koi.

To help you fully understand what your Koi need and why, let's discuss their physical makeup.

Fins are a combination of hard spines, soft filaments, and membrane. Koi have a dorsal fin along the back (1), pectoral (2) and ventral fins (3), which are equivalent to our arms and legs, and caudal/tail fin (4) and anal fins (5), which are used for loco-motion. Two pair of barbels (6) on either side of the mouth are used as sense organs for finding food. Organs along the lateral line are used to sense sounds.

Whether the Koi is scaled or non-scaled, it has a covering referred to as the slime coat. The purpose of the slime coat is to protect it against parasites and diseases.

Although Koi do not have teeth along the jaw line, they do have pharyngeal teeth in three rows behind the tongue. Their purpose is to break up crustaceans or other hard food.

Instead of a stomach, Koi have a very long intestine (about five times the length of the body) that is coiled twice in the abdomen (7) and is connected to the esophagus. A swollen section of the intestine just beyond the esophagus secretes a fluid that breaks down the food. Koi must assimilate their

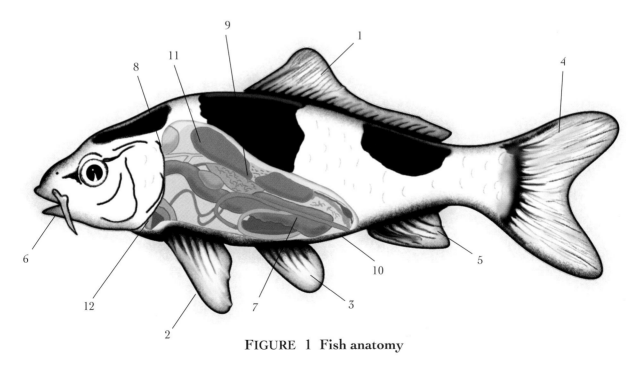

FIGURE 1 Fish anatomy

food quickly and efficiently, since they lack stomachs, where food can be stored for gradual assimilation.

The gills have three important functions: respiration, osmoregulation (maintaining the salt/water balance), and excretion of ammonia. Healthy gills are an absolute must.

Koi have two kidneys. One lies just behind the head (8) and produces white blood cells. The second (9) is located above the swim bladder and is surrounded by capillaries. Waste material in the blood passes through the capillaries to the kidneys, to the pore near the vent (10), and is excreted as urine.

The swim bladder (11) is located in the upper region of the body cavity. Its function is to allow the fish to stay upright and swim with ease. The heart (12) is located close to and beneath the gills, allowing it to pump blood through the gills and then up and back to all the fins, muscles, and organs.

Now, with a better understanding of Koi biology, let's discuss how they should be fed.

What foods to feed, how often, and whether to feed your Koi at all depends entirely on the water temperature of your pond. Water temperature (not air temperature) determines how active the Koi will be and how efficiently they can assimilate the food they are given. Koi are cool-water fish. They do not generate body heat internally; they simulate the temperature of their environment. As the water temperature drops, the internal temperature of Koi drops as well, producing a slowdown in body functions. Therefore, less food is required, because the lower the body temperature of the Koi, the less efficiently the food can be assimilated.

The size and age of the Koi must also be taken into consideration. Young fish grow faster than older ones, and cell building requires more food. A young Koi may eat more that 5% of its body weight daily and may double or triple its size in a few months, provided the water temperature is between 65°F (18°C) and 75°F (24°C).

LENGTH/WEIGHT PROBABILITY CHART

Inches	Ounces
3	0.1 to 0.2
4	0.3 to 0.4
5	0.5 to 0.7
6	1.0 to 1.3
7	1.5 to 1.7
8	2.5 to 3.0
9	4.0 to 5.5
10	5.5 to 7.5

11	7.0 to 10.0
12	10.0 to 14.0
Centimeters	*Grams*
7.67	2.8 to 5.7
10.2	8.5 to 1.3
12.7	14.2 to 19.8
15.2	28.4 to 36.9
17.8	42.5 to 48.2
20.3	70.9 to 85.1
22.9	113.4 to 155.9
25.4	155.9 to 212.6
27.9	198.5 to 283.5
30.5	283.5 to 396.9

PERCENT OF FOOD FOR TOTAL BODY WEIGHT

Age	*Size in Inches*	*Water Temperature*	
		55°F to 65°F	*65°F to 77°F*
UP TO ONE YEAR	1 to 3	1/2 to 1%	3% to 5%
ONE TO THREE YEARS	3 to 5	1/2 to 1%	2% to 3%
OVER THREE YEARS	Over 5	1/2 to 1%	1%

PERCENT OF FOOD FOR TOTAL BODY WEIGHT

Age	*Size in Centimeters*	*Water Temperature*	
		13°C to 18°C	*18°C to 25°C*
UP TO ONE YEAR	2.5 to 7.6	1/2 to 1%	3% to 5%
ONE TO THREE YEARS	7.6 to 12.7	1/2 to 1%	2% to 3%
OVER THREE YEARS	Over 5	1/2 to 1%	1%

Protein is more difficult to break down and excrete than vegetable matter; therefore, the lower the water temperature, the less protein should be fed. The ideal diet for your Koi should vary between a low-protein diet of approximately 35% protein and a high-protein diet of approximately 40% protein. You may also choose to feed your Koi food that includes natural color enhancers, such as spirulina and shrimp. The best-quality foods will include whitefish meal, grains, vitamins, and chelated minerals. Remember when reading the labels that the ingredients are listed in order of content, from the highest to the lowest. In other words, in the best foods you can expect to see fish meal first on the list of ingredients.

The first pellet food your fish should receive in the spring, when they are becoming active and water temperatures are just beginning to warm up, should be low-protein. Feed a low-protein diet in the fall, when lowering water temperatures make Koi less active. If you have a rather small pond and do not want your fish to grow rapidly, a low-protein diet will keep them in good health, but at a slower growth rate.

High-protein diets are fed when Koi are the most active and are designed to maximize the growth and development that occurs when pond temperatures are between 65°F (18°C) and 75°F (24°C). Keep in mind that high-protein foods (fed at proper water temperatures) are also beneficial in preparing Koi for a long winter fast.

Color-enhancing foods are very widely used. However, evidence shows that too much can cause the white on Koi (especially male Koi) to become a very undesirable off-white or yellowish white.

Used in moderation, these foods do enhance colors.

You will find floating pellet food and sinking foods available. The floating foods have two very important advantages. You can readily see if your Koi have been fed more than they want to eat in a reasonable time (10 to 15 minutes). If you feed too much and food is left over, remove it immediately so it does not rot and foul the pond. The second advantage of floating pellets is that they give you the perfect opportunity to examine your Koi when they come up to the surface to eat. Unless you net your Koi, you will not have any other opportunity to check them closely for parasites, wounds, or other problems. Throw the food into the pond close to the edge so you can observe your Koi easily.

When selecting your Koi food, check whether different pellet sizes (*i.e.*, small, medium, and large) are available in each of the desired diets. Most Koi keepers have Koi of varying sizes, making it necessary to feed small pellets so the smallest fish will be able to eat. Large fish simply eat many small pellets. Mixing pellet sizes together is an excellent alternative.

Do not be tempted to buy foods that are low in price and promise fast growth. Many Koi keepers have been convinced that trout chow is a good, inexpensive food, only to find out that the growth rate was so accelerated, their Koi experienced liver damage.

Game fish hatcheries feed these formulas to get the most growth in the least amount of time. Their goal is to have fish of legal size to stock ponds and streams for local sportsmen. Game fish raised in hatcheries are not intended to have long lives. Koi, on the other hand, are our pets, and we want them to live long, healthy lives. Unrefrigerated Koi/goldfish food has a shelf life of approximately six months. So, take into consideration where the food you select is manufactured. Imported foods are not likely to be as fresh, and consequently not as nutritional, as foods manufactured domestically. If you have food left over in the fall, seal it tightly and store in a cold, dry place. Storing it in a freezer until the spring would be ideal.

Koi will eat just about anything we eat. Beef, chicken without bones, shrimp, fish, vegetables, pasta (no sauce, please!), even citrus and cherries.

Since all of these foods will sink to the bottom of your pond, great care must be taken to be sure all the food is eaten or it will foul your pond water. Earthworms are a welcome treat. If you've taught your fish to eat out of your hand, you can control the amount you give them and make sure that everybody gets one. Krill is a wonderful natural color-enhancing, body-building, high-protein food that is a real treat for your Koi. Wheat germ, earthworms, and spirulina are all highly nutritional and easily assimilated.

The following is a suggested feeding schedule we have found very satisfactory.

SPRING AND FALL WATER TEMPERATURES

BELOW 49°F (9°C)	DO NOT FEED	
50° to 54°F (10° to 12°C)	Spinach and collard greens*	Once a week
55° to 60°F (13° to 15°C)	Spinach and collard greens, mixed every other day with a low-protein pellet	Once a day
61° to 65°F (16° to 18°C)	Low-protein pellet	Twice a day
66° to 72°F (19° to 22°C)	High-protein and/or color-enhancing pellet	Three times a day
73° to 76°F (23° to 24°C)	High-protein or color-enhancing pellets or fresh/frozen greens	Four times a day
77° to 86°F (25° to 30°C)	All diets. Greens a.m. and p.m.	Five times a day
Above 86°F (30°C)	DO NOT FEED	

*Frozen chopped spinach and collard greens make a wonderful "slow release" food, high in Vitamin C, and very beneficial to Koi in the spring, after the long winter without food, and in the fall, when you are getting them ready for winter.

When water temperatures dictate that you must not feed Koi, regardless of how hard they may try to convince you they are hungry, DO NOT FEED! Many Koi keepers have not been able to resist feeding when the water temperatures were too cold, and as a result their Koi died. There is no need to worry about your Koi starving. If your pond is functioning properly, you should have algae "fuzz" growing on the sides, which will provide a low-protein diet, easiest of all diets to digest, a source of food for your Koi year-round. If they really need to eat, Koi will happily graze on the algae.

If you live in a seasonal climate, when and what to feed can be very confusing, especially if you experience warm temperatures one week and temperatures below 50°F (10°C) the next. Although your pond temperatures may be fine for feeding one week, when the pond suddenly becomes cold your Koi will not be able to assimilate their food efficiently and excrete their waste. Watch the extended weather reports. If in doubt, feed leafy greens or discontinue feeding altogether and let your Koi take advantage of the high-in-Vitamin C, low-in-protein algae "fuzz" mentioned earlier. To be really safe, stop feeding at water temperatures below 55°F (13°C) or when temperatures are not consistently at safe feeding levels for five or six days at a time.

Another consideration in the spring, when you start feeding your Koi, is your bio-filter. If you leave your filter running all winter as we do, you have some beneficial bacteria available for converting

Chagoi eating an orange

ammonia and nitrites at the beginning of the spring season. However, if you drain, clean, and turn off your bio-filter in the fall, you are starting the season without beneficial bacteria in your filter to handle the conversion of ammonia and nitrites into nitrates. Therefore, although your Koi may be ready for more frequent feedings and a protein food, your bio-filter does not have a bacterial colony ready to handle the fish waste. In this case, begin by feeding sparingly, with foods such as spinach, pastas, and collard greens. You do not want to create a heavy protein waste load when your bio-filter is unable to handle it.

A pond thermometer is very helpful. Be sure to select one that is not made of glass. Look for a thermometer that shows you how often you should be feeding at the temperature registered.

Feeding your Koi properly is of no value if they are living in improperly filtered water. Without clean water, your fish will suffer from poor respiration, poor circulation, and a loss of the slime coat, leaving them vulnerable to diseases and parasites. The chapter on filtration will explain further.

Understanding how your Koi and pond equipment function will allow you to make the right decisions regarding their proper care and maintenance.

Shiro Bekko

CHAPTER THREE

DESIGNING AND PLANNING YOUR POND

HI UTSURI

The first step in planning your pond is to choose the right location. Select a level site in full view of your favorite windows or deck. This will provide you with a constant source of enjoyment and an easy method of observing the safety of the pond and its inhabitants. Build your pond where you spend or would like to spend your leisure time out of doors. You can make your pond an intimate part of your indoor or outdoor living.

Unless there is no other choice, Koi ponds should never be constructed in a full-sun location. Full sun on a pond causes the water to become much warmer than Koi prefer. When Koi are subjected to constant direct sun in clear water, their colors lose their depth and luster. Warm water and sunlight create unsightly algae blooms, which makes it that much more difficult for your bio-filter and UV sterilizer to do their job of keeping your pond water clean and clear. Although Koi like algae, without close monitoring, algae are potentially dangerous during hot weather. Algae are oxygenating plants that put oxygen in the water during the day. However, oxygenating plants also take oxygen out of the water at night. On a hot night the algae can remove so much oxygen from the water, the Koi become oxygen-deprived, suffocate, and die. This happened to a Koi breeder in Japan when he transferred his best female Koi to a green pond during hot weather and neglected to aerate the water properly. Sadly, all the Koi were lost. If a full-sun location is your only option, please consider shading your pond with a lattice arbor, shade cloth, or other creative solution.

Indoor pond

Bringing the outdoors indoors

Latticework provides filtered sunlight for Koi while leaving full sun for lotuses and lilies.

As you can see, the problem can be solved without distracting from the beauty of your pond. Newly treated wood can leach toxic substances into your pond, so be sure to purchase aged wood. Water plants can also be used to provide shade, but if you overdo it you will not be able to see your beautiful Koi.

If you are fortunate to have a site with trees that would provide your pond with filtered sun, be sure to dig your pond far enough away from the trees so you do not weaken their root structure. A tree with a damaged root system can blow over in a storm and take the pond with it.

Now that you have selected the location of your pond, the next consideration is its size and shape. The first pond is always too small! Those cute little fish you buy are going to grow up to be beautiful big fish, and you will never be able to resist buying a new Koi that catches your eye. Build the largest pond you can. You will not be sorry. It is much less expensive to build one large pond than to rebuild a small one.

The authors' informal outdoor pond

If space is limited, be very selective about the Koi you purchase, and maintain a reasonable population. In this way, your pond and Koi will be shown to their best advantage. If you are fortunate enough to have a Koi club in your area, it may prove to be a good source for selling or trading Koi if you need to thin your fish population or if you just want to make room for better ones.

To determine the size and design of your pond, use a garden hose or rope to outline the area you have selected. Keep in mind that you will need working space from every angle of the pond. Step back and compare your outline with the rest of your property. When you are satisfied that the size is in proportion to your landscape, proceed to design the shape. Include in your design an area to handle overflow caused by rain or melting snow. The main thing to remember when determining the shape of your pond is that the water should be free to circulate around all areas. There must never be still water in any part of your pond. Still water becomes stagnant water.

23

The formula for determining the size liner you need to buy for the size pond you have designed is as follows: Measure the length of the pond, add twice the depth, and add 1 foot (30.5 cm) twice, to each side for the overlap. The 1 foot (30.5 cm) overlap is necessary to build a protective edge around the pond, as explained in Chapter 6. Measure the width of the pond, add twice the depth, and add 1 foot (30.5cm) twice to each side for the overlap.

Example: 14′ long × 9′ wide × 2′ deep pond, or a 4.2m long × 2.7m wide × 61 cm deep pond would be calculated as follows:

Length = 14′

Depth = 2′

Overlaps twice

L + 2D + 1′ × 2 = 14′ + 4′ + 2′ = 20′

Width = 9′

Depth = 2′

Overlaps twice

W + 2D + 1′ × 2 = 9′ + 4′ + 2′ = 15′

Therefore, for a 14′ × 9′ × 2′ pond, you would need a 20′ × 15′ liner.

Length = 4.2 m

Depth = 2.7 m

Overlaps twice

L + 2D + 30.5 cm × 2 = 4.2 m + 2 × 2.7 m + 61 cm = 4.2 m + 5.4 m + 0.61 m = 10.21

Width = 9′

Depth = 2′

Overlaps twice

W + 2D + 1′ × 2 = 9 + 4 + 2 = 15′

4.27 m Length + Depth × 2 (1.22 m) + Overlap twice (1.22 m) = 6.1 m

2.75 m Length = Depth × 2 (1.22 m) = Overlap twice (1.22 m) = 4.58 m

Therefore, for a 4.27 m × 2.75 m × .61 cm pond, you would need a 6.1 m × 4.58 m liner.

You may want to consider adding a bog for additional plants or have a natural-looking stream spilling into the pond. Each of these features will give added filtration, and the stream will provide greater aeration, which is always welcome. If you decide to include a bog, remember, no still water.

Planning the depth of your pond is as important as its size and shape. Two feet deep (60 cm) is considered a minimum depth in areas where temperatures can be very cold or very hot. If your pond is large enough and your local ordinances allow, start with two feet (60 cm) and gradually go to a depth of three feet (90 cm) or more. The colder or hotter the climate, the deeper the pond should be. A deeper pond also provides additional exercise for larger Koi.

Next, choose your plant shelf areas. They should be 12″ (30.5 cm) deep and wide enough to accommodate your plant pots and wall stone, at least 20″ (50 cm). Place shelves where the plants will create a nice landscape in the pond without blocking your view of the Koi.

After you have chosen the site and designed your pond, your next step is to buy the right materials and equipment to ensure that your beautiful pond functions properly. Your goals are to have clear water, so you can see your Koi from all angles (including the bottom of the pond) and clean, ammonia- and nitrite-free water. The only algae in your pond should be a slight growth around the sides of the pond, which the Koi can graze on.

The first item to purchase is your pond liner. Plastic, EPDM rubber, and butyl rubber are all available in different thicknesses (mil). Although 32-mil plastic has been used for years, its stiffness makes it very difficult to install, which is a big drawback. Too many folds are necessary to make this type of liner mold to the shape of the pond, and folds provide a hiding place for disease-causing anaerobic bacteria. There are many attractive, successful ponds constructed with this type of liner, but we cannot not give it our recommendation.

EPDM rubber is made from a polymer (ethylene propylene diene monomer polymer). We prefer the 45 mil. Higher mils are very heavy and are cumbersome to work with in large sizes. Unless heavy boulders are included in your pond design, 65 mil is an unnecessary expense. This material is highly resistant to heat, air pollution, and UV rays from the sun. EPDM rubber is very pliable, especially if it is warmed in the sun before being installed, which greatly reduces the number of folds needed to arrive at the shape you have planned for your pond.

Butyl rubber is made from butyl polymer. Its primary use is for waterproofing in protected environments under earth or water, where long-term durability is essential. Butyl is more flexible than plastic or EPDM and much more expensive.

IMPORTANT: Certain curing compounds and fillers commonly used in butyl and EPDM rubber used for roofing are toxic to aquatic life. Never, under any circumstances, use a roofing rubber product. Fish-safe EPDM and butyl come with a guarantee stating they can be used in fish ponds. Never use a swimming-pool liner. These liners are usually treated with algae-killing chemicals that will kill your fish and plants.

A bio-filter is an absolute must for ponds containing fish, be they Koi or goldfish. The features to look for in a bio-filter are high efficiency and low maintenance. Filtration is so essential to the success of a pond that we are devoting an entire chapter to the subject, and we urge you to give it special attention.

An ultraviolet sterilizer (UV sterilizer) is a very desirable piece of equipment to have for your pond. In conjunction with your bio-filter, a UV sterilizer, when properly installed and maintained, will help keep your pond clear of algae at all times.

Stone for the perimeter and sides of the pond can be purchased by the pallet in varying colors at most garden centers. Most garden centers will deliver to your door.

One pump at the correct number of gallons per hour (GPH) can power your bio-filter, UV sterilizer, waterfall, venturi, and fountain(s). A submersible pump that contains non-toxic food-grade oil, or one that can also run from outside the pond, or a magnetic-drive pump, are the most desirable.

To determine the correct pump for your pond, choose one that corresponds to your bio-filtration needs. If you want more power for fountains or waterfalls, either use a separate pump or bypass the flow of a larger pump to operate the bio-filter, and

A formal approach to pond design

use the rest of the flow for your fountain or water-fall. Recirculate your pond every two to four hours. If your pond is 500 gallons (1900 liters), a 250 GPH (950 LPH) pump is needed. If the same pond is using a pump that is 250 GPH (950 LPH) at one foot (30 cm) and you are pumping up five feet (1.5 m), a larger pump is needed. The higher the elevation, the more power you need to get the desired GPH/LPH.

If you use tubing to connect your pumps to the filter, UV sterilizer, fountain, or other equipment, buy black tubing rather than clear. Black tubing is much less obvious, prevents algae growth inside the tube, and can be easily camouflaged.

After reading the chapter on pond building, you may want to include a vortex settlement chamber,

Formal Japanese-style pond and teahouse

skimmer, bottom drain, venturi, and other enhancements. Each of these features makes a more efficient pond. However, you can have a successful pond with just a good bio-filter, pump, and a UV sterilizer. The difference is in the additional maintenance required.

CHAPTER FOUR

FILTRATION

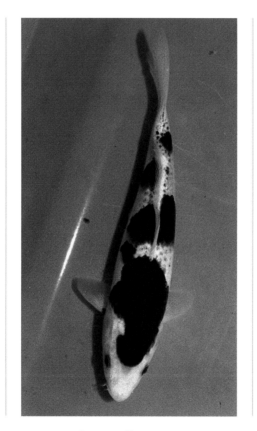

BUDO SANKE

Orenji-Hariwake

ty of any garden. Even worse, not giving your pond the benefit of a good bio-filter means making your Koi live in their own wastes. Someone is going to tell you that he has had a pond without bio-filtration and it is doing fine. Maybe at present it is fine, but ponds change constantly.

A friend of ours had ponds for three or four years without filtration. Her Koi grew and spawned and, as we all do, she added new Koi to her collection every year. Each of these changes seriously affected the balance of her pond, until what every Koi keeper fears happened to our friend. The ammonia and nitrite levels in her pond spiked to dangerous levels and she lost many of her precious Koi. It was a lesson for all of us. It is vital to your success as a Koi keeper to understand how bio-filtration works. Once you do, you will be able to maintain a healthy pond and healthy Koi.

PROPER BIO-FILTRATION IS THE KEY TO SUCCESSFUL KOI KEEPING

In natural bodies of water, ammonia and nitrite from fish wastes and rotting vegetation are converted into less toxic nitrates by aerobic bacteria. Aerobic bacteria need water flow and aeration to prosper. To build a pond is to create a closed system that needs help to function like a natural pond with water flowing in and out constantly. Ammonia and nitrites create two problems for Koi. Ammonia is very damaging to fish gills. Even low levels of ammonia over an extended period of time will burn gills beyond repair and kill Koi. Nitrites are very tox-

THE KEY TO SUCCESSFUL KOI KEEPING

Why is filtering a Koi pond so important? It is essential if your Koi are to live a long, healthy life, and if you want to be able to see them in your beautiful *"gin,"* clear pond. A dirty, pea green pond certainly does not add to the beau-

ic, especially to small Koi. The dangerous nature of these two toxins, plus the fact that they are a nutrient for algae, presents a twofold problem when ammonia and nitrite are in the pond, *i.e.*, fish are in danger of burned gills, disease due to physical damage, and oxygen deprivation, which occurs because algae remove excessive amounts of oxygen from ponds on hot nights.

Bio-filtration is the establishment of the nitrogen cycle. The main steps in this cycle are shown in the following drawing, illustrating the conversion of the waste products of ammonia and nitrite to the less toxic form of nitrate. The process is a constant, ever balancing cycle. The aerobic bacteria colony in your bio-filter will grow larger with an increase of waste and will diminish with a decrease of waste. Always think of your bio-filter as a living thing and treat it accordingly

Unlike aerobic bacteria, anaerobic bacteria are very toxic to fish. Disease-causing anaerobic bacteria can grow in places where there is no flow of oxygen-rich water, such as in plant pots without a

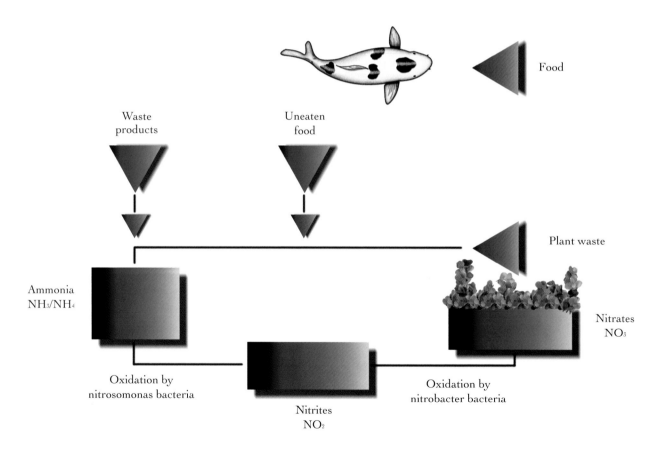

Food

Waste products

Uneaten food

Plant waste

Ammonia
NH₃/NH₄

Nitrates
NO₃

Oxidation by
nitrosomonas bacteria

Oxidation by
nitrobacter bacteria

Nitrites
NO₂

FIGURE 2 Nitrogen cycle

mesh construction, folds in the pond liner, uncirculating water area in a poorly designed pond, and in bio-filters that have areas without proper water flow and oxygen.

Your goal is to provide the best possible environment in which you can cultivate an aerobic bacteria colony large enough to convert the ammonia and nitrite produced by your Koi and plant material.

Since the very beginning of Koi keeping as a hobby, the perfect bio-filter has been the quest of every Koi keeper. Because many older methods of bio-filtration are still being used, it's good to know how some of the more popular ones work.

Over the years there has been a great deal of experimentation, and it continues today. Up-flow, down-flow, or lateral flow, and the use of large or small pebbles became the topic of conversation among Koi keepers all over the world. In our opinion, the advantages of one system over the others are very minimal; however, the lateral flow does have a slight edge over the up- or down-flow.

In a down-flow system, the heavier waste sits on the top of the filter material. The water, therefore, flows constantly through the accumulating waste. This situation can cause clogging, leaving only a few channels where the water can flow through the filter. This greatly limits the area where the aerobic bacteria can colonize and do their work.

In an up-flow system, there should be a sump at the bottom, separated from the filter material, where the heavier waste remains until drained off. This system also channels.

In a lateral system, there should be a solid block of water flowing through the entire system. The heavier waste should drop down to a series of grooves at the bottom of the filter, carrying it to a sump, which can be drained off periodically. This will leave the filter material free of heavy waste, allowing the bio-filter's function to be mainly biological.

The addition of a vortex settlement chamber to any of these systems helps remove heavier waste before it reaches the bio-chamber.

Containers for filters are another source of controversy among hobbyists. Plastic barrels and trash receptacles, as well as boxes and chambers of plastic, treated lumber, or concrete and liner material have been used. Chamber after chamber has been lined with materials such as plastic hair curlers, bio-balls, pebbles, and brushes. One hobbyist told us he used all these materials because he didn't know which one(s) would work. Not very scientific, but this persistent experimentation over the years by the hobbyists has brought us to where we are today. We have certainly learned what doesn't work and what is inefficient. Some hobbyists have made their bio-filters out of hard-shell ponds (preformed plastic ponds) almost the size of the Koi pond. They were following an early theory, based on the use of gravel as a medium, that the filter must be one-third the size of the pond. With today's technology, this is no longer necessary.

As Koi keeping progressed, new and unique methods of bio-filtration developed, especially in the materials used. Because of its large volume but small surface area, gravel was replaced by lava rock. Lava's tiny holes and dimpled surfaces created thousands of minute crevices for aerobic bacteria to colonize. Although lava rock had a much larger surface area, it was still an inert solid mass. Another problem was the eventual channeling caused by a sludge build-up within the core, causing the water to flow in only a few channels rather than through the entire filtering system. Cleaning the sludge out of a lava rock is an involved and unpleasant task because of the lava's weight and sharp edges. This all said, lava is our second choice for filter material.

People have experimented with:

1. Canterbury spar (a crushed gravel)

2. Coke and lytag (coal by-products)

3. Perlag (similar to lytag)

4. Flocor (plastic wire harness cut into small tubes)

5. Plastic pot scrubbers and the mesh bags they come in

6. Hair curlers

7. Plastic toys

8. Foam (man-made sponge)

9. Air-conditioner filters (the material they are made of and the coatings used on them make them very toxic)

10. Siporex (a product made by firing a mixture of sand and salt and then rinsing out the salt to create a porous glass)

11. Anything that will allow aerobic bacteria to colonize

From plastics manufacturers came various forms of bio-balls and numerous configurations of plastic looking like spheres, columns, stars, and other forms to which "good" bacteria could adhere. Bio-balls are light and easily cleaned; however, they have a lot of void spaces due to the openness of the forms.

Zeolite (a hydrous silicate) products, which act as ion exchangers, were thought to be useful in ponds. This has proven to be incorrect since they only function for a short period of time, and they do not convert ammonia, they absorb it. Once saturated, zeolite products need to be recharged by being soaked in a salt solution that removes the ammonia. Some hobbyists are being advised to used zeolite in conjunction with their bio-filters as a safeguard against ammonia build-up. Think about this. When zeolite absorbs ammonia, it deprives the aerobic bacteria colony of nutrition that would increase the colony's growth. Therefore, when the zeolite becomes saturated and can no longer absorb any more ammonia, the entire ammonia load is immediately passed on to a bio-filter that has not colonized to the point where it is able to convert the extra load of ammonia. We would never use zeolite or any zeolite product in our pond system. It may be fine for aquariums, but in our opinion it is not for ponds.

Charcoal is another aquarium-friendly product that Koi keepers have been told would be advantageous, but it presents the same absorption and recharging problem as zeolite. Again, it absorbs; it does not convert. There are so-called bio-filters available that have nothing in them but zeolite and charcoal. They will not convert ammonia and nitrites.

Brushes are another type of filter material. They work well for mechanical filtration and can have some biological action. On the downside, in recent years it has been discovered that the close spacing of the bristles at the center of the spiral wire that is used to hold them in the correct configuration can be conducive to the formation of disease-causing anaerobic bacteria.

Using vegetation for filtration is a very useful method for supplementing a working bio-system. It is not advisable to use plants as the exclusive source of filtration. In natural ponds many plants aid in filtration. However, a constant flow of water carries the waste downstream through miles of sand, gravel, vegetation and such until it finally reaches the sea. In a closed system such as your pond, the same water must recycle. In this situation, vegetation assists in the nitrogen cycle by getting nourishment from nitrogen produced from dissolved nitrites. We definitely encourage you to include plants in your pond. Plants are beneficial and decorative. But if your goal is to use only plants to filter your pond, you will have so many plants you will not be able to see your Koi. There are other downsides to too many plants. The plant parts that do not continue to grow break down and add waste products to the pond. Oxygenating plants (leaves under the water) add oxygen to the water during the day, which is very good for your Koi. These same oxygenating plants (which include algae) reverse the process during the night and take oxygen out of the water, which is not good for your Koi. If you have too many oxygenating plants and algae in your pond, during a hot spell your pond could be dangerously depleted of its oxygen supply and you would lose your Koi. As with most things, moderation is best.

A system that has been highly engineered to accomplish all the necessary functions and is the easiest to maintain is a pre-filter vortex settlement chamber, which will mechanically remove the heavy waste material prior to its introduction to the bio-filter. This alleviates the load on the filter material, allows easy cleaning, and eliminates the problem of the bio-filter becoming clogged with debris.

The most desirable bio-filter is one that is engineered so that:

1. the water eddies evenly throughout the entire system, leaving no areas without water flow where disease-causing anaerobic bacteria can grow;

2. the water flow provides oxygen to assist in the growth of the aerobic bacteria colony;

3. the heavy waste drops down to a series of grooves and into a sump that can be drained.

Filter pads (our preferred filter material) are best if made of an extruded plastic material of just the right denier to provide the aerobic bacteria an almost unlimited area for colonization without the solid mass of a larger denier and without causing the clogging problem of a smaller denier. You should be able to clean the pads in the bio-filter by simply stopping the flow with valves and/or turning off the pump, rinsing the filter pads in the pond water and draining out the unwanted dirty water. If you have water that is not chlorinated (well water) you can rinse the filter pads with a garden hose. Chlorinated water will kill the bacteria colony. Rinsing in the pond water or flushing it with the garden hose will not dislodge the colony. If you have chlorinated water, dechlorinate some water and rinse the pads. Finding a dechlorinating product should not be a problem. Most dealers carry them.

Design your filtration system in a way that allows the pump to be attached outside the pond to the discharge end of the filter. This will provide easy access to your pump for maintenance.

Since the water is filtered before it enters the pump chamber in this type of filtration design, the pump impeller will last longer and the pump screen will not become clogged. (See Figure 17.)

Let us assume that you have selected your bio-filter, installed it, turned it on, and it is ready to do its work. Now what? Well, it can't cultivate a bacteria colony without fish waste to nourish it, and your Koi cannot thrive unless your bio-filter is colonized. Don't panic. There is an easy solution. Buy one of the many bacteria start-up products, follow the instructions, and add it to your pond accordingly. As with any product, some are better than others. Look for one that is highly concentrated. If the bacteria comes in a large container, it will

Ever-Flo bio-filter (open)

Ever-Flo bio-filter (closed)

take a lot to get your filter going. On the other hand, if the container and dosage are both small, the product is very concentrated. In our travels, we have found that professional fish hatcheries use concentrated products, so we decided to give one a try. After years of pouring huge amounts of bacteria into the pond every spring to help get things going, it was a blessing to get the filter going quickly and efficiently. The added bonus, of course, was that it cost much less to use the concentrated product.

How do you know if your bio-filter is working and your pond water is ammonia- and nitrite-free? Test the water! With a new pond system, it is crucial to test the pond water every day to see where the ammonia and nitrite levels are! Ammonia, nitrite, and nitrate test kits are readily available almost everywhere. Given a choice between liquid tests and dry-tab tests, we recommend the liquid, which are much faster and very accurate. It will take at least four to six weeks even with adding bacteria to the pond before your pond water gets past the first algae bloom and your water is free of toxins. Partial water changes will be necessary in order to dilute the toxicity. Once your bio-filter is functioning properly, you should continue to take tests at least once a week. Remember, your bio-filter will be challenged with changes every day of one kind or another. Don't wait until you have disease in your pond or you start to lose Koi before testing your water quality. Preventing a disaster is much easier and less heartbreaking than cleaning up after it happens. The efficiency of your bio-filter is paramount to the health of your Koi. Koi keeping is all about water quality. Once you accept, understand, and apply that knowledge, you will have the key to successful Koi keeping.

ULTRAVIOLET STERILIZERS

TAISHO SANKE

The most frequently asked question by pond owners is "How do I get rid of the algae?" Even in a pond with a great bio-filter, conditions such as hot weather, direct sun, overfeeding, and other factors can cause algae blooms periodically. There are basically three options. Algaecides are available and they do kill algae, by removing the oxygen from the water. If that sounds scary, it should. If you do not know exactly how many gallons of water are in your pond, you have no idea how much algaecide to use to treat the pond without removing so much oxygen from the water that you not only kill the algae, you kill your plants and your Koi as well. Another option is products that gather the algae into a mass that drops to the bottom of the pond. These products work but make a mess and clog up the filter system. Or, you can invest in an ultraviolet sterilizer. This is definitely our choice.

In the past the Koi-keeping community was reluctant to accept the safety and usefulness of ultraviolet sterilizers. Its fear was that the ponds would be sterile and the Koi would be so disease- and parasite-free that their immune systems would break down. Fortunately, this theory has been proven incorrect and discarded. There are so many outside influences on a pond that it would be impossible to keep it sterile.

Ultraviolet sterilizers are used in hot tubs and spas to eliminate the need for large amounts of chlorine to keep the water clean. In the food industry they are used to purify liquids such as milk. Tropical fish hobbyists have successfully used them for years in their aquariums. Hospitals use them for sterilizing certain instruments and areas in the hospital. Fish hatcheries use them to sterilize their source water before it enters the systems used to raise large numbers of fry (newly hatched fish). With all of this evidence, it stands to reason that UV sterilizers would be beneficial to a Koi pond.

It is now commonly accepted that ultraviolet sterilizers are definitely an asset to Koi keeping. They keep pond water clear by eliminating waterborne algae, and they reduce the populations of viruses, bacteria, protozoa, and fungi that may be present in your pond. In other words, they assist you in your quest for a clear, healthy pond and beautiful, healthy Koi.

The technical description of the function of a UV sterilizer is: A shortwave ultraviolet light that reduces the population of waterborne microorganisms, provided they are exposed to the light long enough to break down the DNA chain, thus preventing the microorganism from reproducing.

To accomplish this, the flow rate (or dwell time) is determined by the intensity of the lamp in direct relationship to the flow of water. The killing power is a little different with each manufacturer. Our UV sterilizer manufacturer recommends the following formula:

15,000 units to kill algae;

30,000 units to kill bacteria;

45,000 units to kill protozoa (parasites) and fungi.

To obtain the proper units, either increase the wattage or slow the water flow by one-half or one-third, and you will get the same results.

UV WATT SIZE TO KILL

Pond Gals	Pump GPH	50/50 Split GPH	Recycles per Day	A	A/B	A/B/P
500	250	125	6	12W	25W	25W
1000	500	250	6	25W	40W	40W
2000	1000	500	6	40W	65W	65W
3000	1500	750	6	40W	65W	130W
4000	2000	1000	6	65W	130W	130W
5000	2500	1250	6	65W	130W	195W

You can use less wattage by using the following chart as your guide.

UV SIZE TO KILL

Pond Gals	Pump GPH	Valve Flow GPH	Recycles per Day	A	A/B	A/B/P
500	250	83	4	12W	12W	25W
1000	500	167	4	12W	25W	40W
2000	1000	333	4	25W	40W	65W
3000	1500	500	4	40W	65W	65W
4000	2000	666	4	40W	65W	130W
5000	2500	833	4	65W	30W	130W

A = Algae; B = Bacteria; P = Protozoa

Your dealer should be able to give you the manufacturer's recommended flow rate for their UV sterilizers. Following their recommendation and keeping your UV running constantly during warm weather (above freezing), will keep your pond clear of algae and reduce the microorganisms to a low level. In this environment, your Koi will use their immune systems for protection from those dangers that may remain.

Plumbing for proper flow can be accomplished several ways. We suggest:

1. Attach a reducing tee to the pump discharge with the flow directed to the stem of the tee. Connect the smallest outlet of the reducing tee to the UV sterilizer. Now plumb the remaining outlet on the tee to a waterfall, fountain, pond, or other device.

2. Install a valve on the discharge side of the pump after a full (not reduced) tee.

3. Use a separate pump with a control valve and filter for the UV sterilizer.

4. Plumb the UV sterilizer with a control valve on the gravity flow side of your filter.

Your UV sterilizer should always be attached after the bio-filter to reduce the amount of debris flowing through it. This will also reduce interference with the biological action of the filter. Aerobic bacteria flowing through the UV sterilizer would be damaged before it could get to your bio-filter and colonize.

The quality of the glass used in the quartz sleeves and bulbs in a UV sterilizer is very important to the efficiency of the unit you purchase. The purpose of the quartz sleeve is to maintain the temperature for maximum output when water temperatures are below 72°F (22°C). Since UV sterilizers are being manufactured all over the world and new claims of efficiency abound, the best advice is to read the material that comes with the UV you are considering and discuss it thoroughly with your dealer. Only purchase a UV sterilizer if you are completely satisfied that the manufacturer has provided complete information and that your dealer is knowledgeable enough to provide any needed assistance.

Keep your UV sterilizer clean. Your sterilizer must be clean to be efficient. Dirty water and dirt on the sleeve block the UV light, which in turn greatly reduces its power and efficiency. Check the condition of the unit on a regular basis. If you live in a seasonal climate you will need to store your UV indoors when temperatures begin to get down to the freezing point. Before storing, clean it with bleach and rinse thoroughly with clean water.

Don't run your UV sterilizer when first starting up the pond. Let your bio-filter get balanced before turning on the sterilizer. You want all of the aerobic bacteria to have a chance to colonize.

The approximate life of a UV bulb is 9,000 hours. Just because the light is on does not mean it is functioning. We live in a region with four seasons, so it is very easy for us to determine when we need a new bulb. Every spring we put in a new one. If you live in a region where the temperature is above freezing all year round, you will need to do some calculating.

We have run our pond with and without a UV sterilizer, and we would never again have a pond without one. Just be sure your UV sterilizer and all the other electrical connections to the pond are attached to a ground-fault interrupter circuit that is either mounted in your breaker box or mounted on a properly wired individual outlet.

HOW TO BUILD A LINER POND

HARIWAKE

Carefully choose a site that conforms to the guidelines previously covered in Chapter Three, "Designing & Planning Your Pond." Mark out the perimeter with either a garden hose or a rope. If you wish to see stone rather than liner when looking into your pond, you must lay wall stone from a shelf 13 inches (33 cm) down from the top of the proposed water level. To accomplish this, excavate the area you have outlined, digging a 20° slant inward to a depth of 13 inches (33 cm) from the final water level and a width of 20 inches (51 cm), which will allow 12 inches (30.5 cm) for the plant shelf and 8 inches (20.5 cm) for the wall stone. Digging the side of your pond at a 20° slant will ease the pressure if ice forms on your pond (Figure 3).

Your plant shelves should be on the side(s) opposite the waterfall and/or spillway. When your plants are on the shelves, they will create a decorative safety barrier between your Koi and any predators that might come along. The wall stone extending down into the water will give your pond a lovely, natural look.

Next, excavate the area where you have planned a waterfall and/or spillway to a depth of 12 inches (30.5 cm) and 8 inches (20.5 cm) wide. There will not be a plant shelf in this area; therefore, you only need to allow 8 inches (20.5 cm) for the wall stone. When this is complete, dig down to the bottom level. Remove the bottom soil to a depth of 24 inches (61 cm) or more, depending on your temperate zone or desire for a deeper pond (Figure 4).

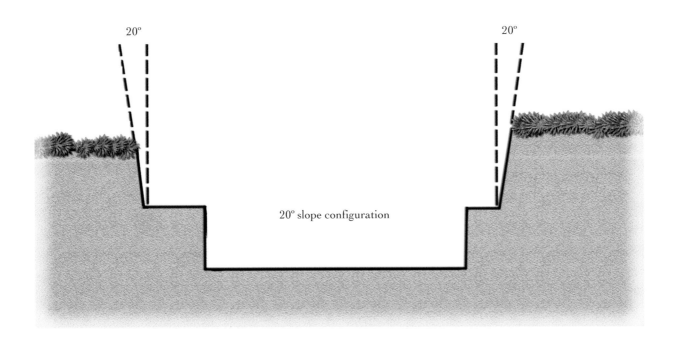

FIGURE 3 Pond with plant shelf

Please check your local ordinances regarding the depth of your pond. Make sure all upper elevations are level and the bottom is pitched away from the waterfall/spillway to the area chosen for a bottom drain or sump area that will be used for periodic cleaning. With some of the excavated soil, build a slight rise on the outer edge of the pond and above the existing ground level to prevent rainwater, mud, and lawn and garden chemicals from draining into the pond.

If you do not want a plant shelf or decide to have the liner come all the way up to the edge of the pond, dig a small depression at the desired level around the rim of the pond to hold the wall stone, brick, pavers, or whatever you are using as a finishing edge. Tuck the liner up behind the edge so that rain cannot carry dirt and garden chemicals into the water (Figure 5).

There are several choices in locating the bio-filter: in the pond, above pond level (neither of these is the best choice, in our opinion), or at pond level. The plumbing is a little different for each configuration. Our idea of a perfect filtration system is one that:

1. is easily hidden

2. is easy to maintain

3. is installed at pond level

4. has a vortex settlement chamber

5. is fed from a bottom drain(s), side intake(s) and skimmer(s)

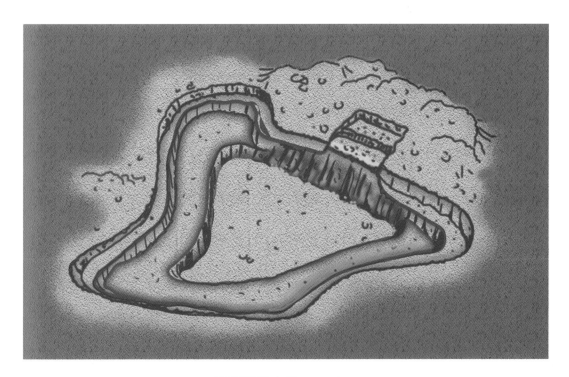

FIGURE 4 Excavation

41

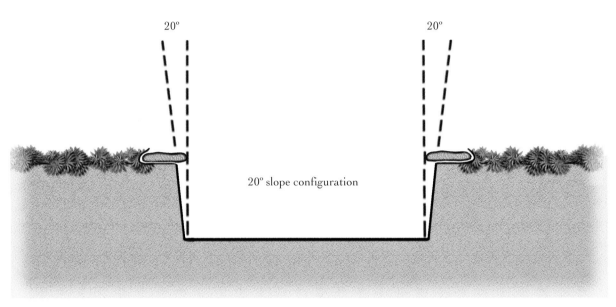

20° 20°

20° slope configuration

FIGURE 5 Pond without plant shelf

6. has plumbing of 2-inch (5 cm), or larger, flexible tubing throughout

7. is powered with a dependable pump with sufficient horsepower for the correct flow of the system

8. includes an ultraviolet sterilizer

9. is valve-controlled to turn off any part of the system for maintenance, cleaning, and winterizing

10. includes a venturi for aeration

11. has an overflow for seasonal rain and snow

12. has an automatic fill valve

13. includes a low-water alarm

14. has a strong pond cover that is easily placed and removed

To install a bottom drain for cleaning and filtering the debris from the bottom, dig a small trench and pipe it beyond the outer edge of the pond to a valve location. Install the valve and shut it for now. Follow the bottom drain installation instructions carefully, making sure when the pond is completed that the drain will be positioned to allow waste to run into it. Be sure to tamp the soil under the drain so that settling does not pull the drain too far down and stretch the lining. Run the drain either to a lower part of the garden, to a French drain, or to a barrel with a sump pump. Install a valve to control runoff for draining or cut off to do filter maintenance (Figure 6).

A swimming pool–type skimmer with a leaf basket is another plus in planning your pond. It will capture leaves, pollen and other floating debris. To determine the best location for your skimmer, look

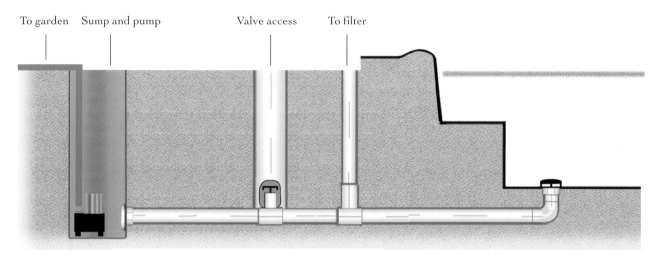

To garden   Sump and pump   Valve access   To filter

FIGURE 6 Bottom drain

at your trees, shrubs, and fence (if you have one) and note where the wind has blown debris. Locate your skimmer on the side of the pond that will collect wind-driven debris. The natural movement of the air currents will sweep across the surface and deposit the debris into the skimmer. The plumbing on this can be connected to the midpoint intake or a separate line. However, you should install valves on the bottom of the skimmer and direct the flow to the filter or to a drain. If temperatures go below freezing, drain your pond to a level below the bottom of the skimmer. Drain and plug your skimmer to prevent rain from getting inside and freezing, which could cause the skimmer to crack (Figure 7).

Recently a new floating type of skimmer has become available. The advantage of this skimmer is that it automatically adjusts to the water level. Also, it can be easily disconnected and plugged

during freezing weather, eliminating the need to drop the pond water down below the skimmer (Figure 8).

Another pond maintenance feature to consider installing is a mid-depth intake that will draw water from the midpoint of the pond. Install it with a bulkhead large enough to draw a sufficient amount of water into the bio-filter (Figure 9).

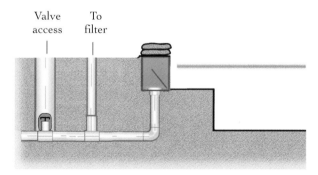

Valve   To
access   filter

FIGURE 7 Swimming pool–type skimmer

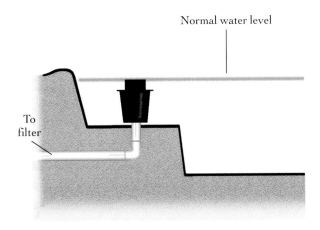

FIGURE 8 Floating skimmer

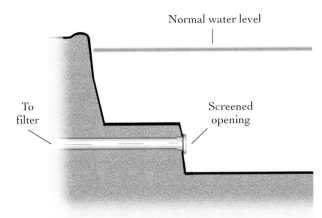

FIGURE 9 Mid-depth intake

The common size for outlets on skimmers and bottom drains is 1 1/2 inches (38 mm). For increased efficiency, increase the outlets to 2 inches (5 cm) by attaching and clamping 2 inch (5 cm) flexible hose to the external threads. The advantage of flexible hose is that it does not crack like fixed plumbing if there is any settling of the plumbing or filtration system.

Snow and rain can cause a disastrous overflow if allowed to run out wherever the lowest edge of the pond happens to be. To avoid this situation, install an overflow device. Lay a pipe in the pond and/or filtration system where the overflow is directed out to a discharge area of your choice. Figures 10, 11, and 12 show three possible solutions.

After all of these options have been addressed, level the top of the excavation and smooth all areas (Figure 13).

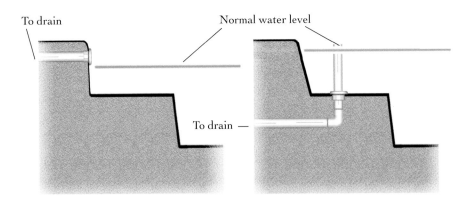

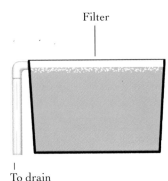

FIGURES 10, 11, 12 Overflow choices

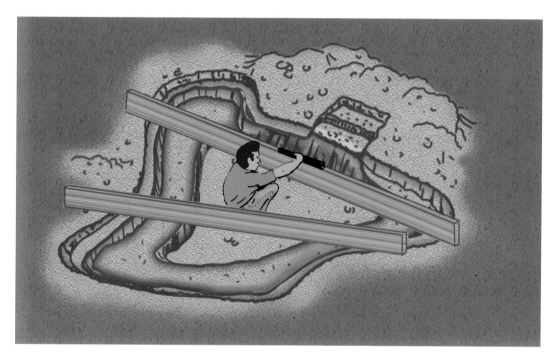

FIGURE 13 Pond excavation leveling

Remove all rocks, pebbles, roots, and other possible hazards to the liner. Cover the excavation with a commercial underliner. Some underlining material is needle-punched. Sometimes the needles break off and puncture the liner under the pressure of the water, so avoid this type. A good underliner will prevent rocks, roots, and other items from puncturing the liner. It will also stop burrowing animals from chewing a hole in the liner, something old carpeting or newspaper will not do. Cover the underliner with a heavy liner. Ideally, you have selected a butyl or EPDM liner, a 30-mil. (1 mil = .001″, one thousandth of an inch) butyl or a 40- or 45-mil EPDM. In either case, be sure it is guaranteed fish-safe and is not roofing rubber.

If you have chosen a pond size that is larger than a standard-size liner, be sure it is factory-constructed or seamed. Field seaming is not as stable as a factory seam. A hot-bonding process using an expensive machine provides a seam that is as strong as the rubber itself. Cold-tape seams are weaker than the rubber sheeting; however, they will work well for areas of the liner that are not under stress. A good example would be waterfalls, which can be made from scrap material left over from the job. Cold-tape seams work well in this application. Do not use contact adhesives. They are too weak and do not have sufficient resistance to pond water. Also, contact adhesives may contain chemicals that are toxic to fish. For any type of seaming, the liner must first be cleaned with the proper solvents. Use either white gasoline, such as Coleman fuel, or

45

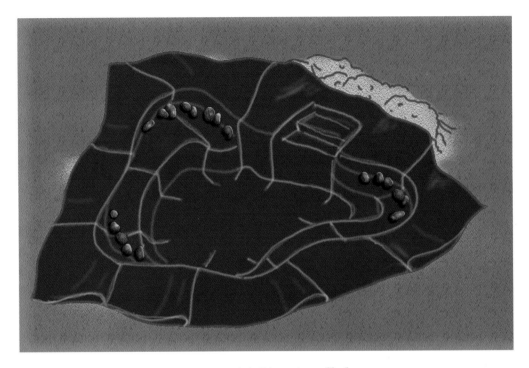

FIGURE 14 Liner installed

toluene, which can be obtained at hardware stores.

When the bottom and sides of the excavation are covered with the underliner you are ready to install your liner. Unfold or unroll the liner close to the pond. Pull it across the pond and give it a little flip to allow air under it. Then let it float into position. When the liner is in place and the folds have been carefully made, lay the outer edge of the liner over the raised outer edges of the pond and secure by placing the stones around the edge. DO NOT TRIM THE EXCESS FROM AROUND THE EDGES (Figure 14).

If you installed a bottom drain, screw the plate into the base and tighten. Then cut the hole.

Install your midway intake(s) with bulkhead(s) (see Figure 9) and pipe them to their valve posi-tions. The remainder of the plumbing can be finished later.

To install the skimmer(s), make sure the top of the skimmer intake is about two inches (5 cm) above the water level. Secure the faceplate around the liner before cutting the opening. Plumb this in tan-dem with the side intake or separately. Place the valves so the skimmer can be plugged and drained for freezing temperature hookup. For the new float-ing skimmer, plumb it into a side intake.

Now you are ready to continue laying the wall stone. Start at the point below the waterfall and/or spillway and continue around and upwards, plac-ing the stone over the liner on the outer edge.

Complete building up the wall from the shelves to at least 6 inches (15 cm) higher than ground

FIGURE 15 Complete pond configuration

level. With the liner securely in place, slowly run water into the pond. Straighten the overlapping liner around the edge and trim, leaving at least 12 inches (30 cm). Place your stone around the edge of the pond in an unstable manner to discourage predators such as raccoons and cats (Figure 15).

For the waterfall, build up the area with the soil removed from the pond excavation, building either steps or a slope. Cover with strips of liner, making sure to overlap the strips to prevent leakage, as shown (Figure 16a). Lay stone along the liner following your configuration of choice, keeping the

Liner overlapping

Stones overlapping

FIGURE 16a, b Waterfall configurations

liner up between the stone to confine the water. Add some stones to give the water a pleasant sound and to aerate it as it bubbles down the slope. If you are using steps, have the upper stones overhang the lower ones (Figure 16b).

Remember: the sound of a waterfall is as important as its appearance.

If you are using all the components suggested, complete your filtration system as shown in Figure 17.

Your next step is to plumb in your ultraviolet sterilizer. The discharge of the UV goes to any of the following choices: venturi for aerating your pond,

fountain to provide aeration and beauty, or waterfall or spillway. The only critical point here is the proper flow through the sterilizer. This will be accomplished with tees or valves to obtain the necessary flow rate as discussed in the chapter on UV sterilizers.

The vortex and bio-filter should have drains for removing heavy waste and dirt. Design an easy access by placing a large piece of pipe directly over the valve so it can be operated from above. Either a ball, gate or knife valve is acceptable (Figure 18).

When the plumbing is completed, allow the dirt created by construction to settle in the pond.

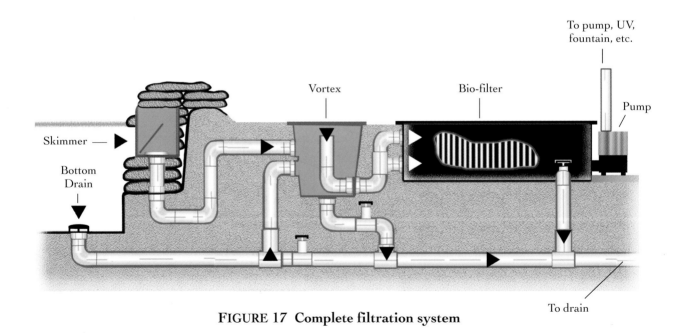

FIGURE 17 Complete filtration system

Then drain the water, clean the pond, and refill. Time your water supply by filling a gallon container (or a container of a standard measure where you are) and observing the time it takes to fill. Ours takes 20 seconds (3 gallons per minute). Then place the hose in the pond and time how long it takes to fill. To get an accurate calculation, avoid running water for other purposes until the pond is filled. When the water has reached the desired level note the time again. This will give you the exact number of gallons of water in your pond, which is critical information. You need this information in order to properly treat your pond and/or your Koi. For example: if it took 4 hours and 47 minutes to fill, it would take 287 minutes × 3 gallons per minute = 861 gallons. If you have a pond with no shelves, one depth, and squared, not rounded, your formula would be Length × Depth × Width × 7.5 = number of U.S. gallons.

Your pond is now constructed, but it is still too soon to introduce your Koi. Let the pond run for a few days to make sure there are no leaks and that all of the plumbing is working correctly.

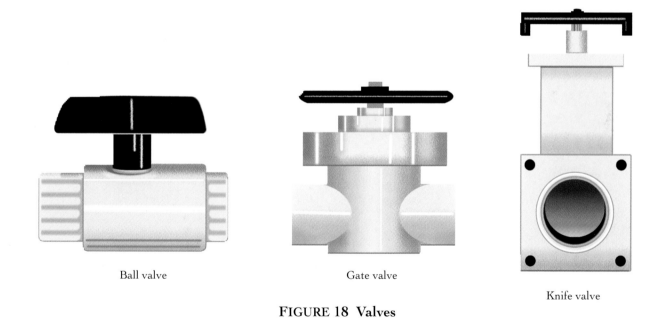

Ball valve

Gate valve

Knife valve

FIGURE 18 Valves

NEW POND
START-UP

GINRIN TANCHO KOHAKU

After you have installed the liner, completed the plumbing, connected the ground-fault electrical system and filled your pond, it is time to turn it on. Do not put Koi in the pond just yet. First, test everything for leaks or overflow. Are you satisfied with the way the waterfall looks and sounds? Be sure the water comes from and goes to each area as designed. Let it run a day or so and continue to check for leaks or overflow.

Once you are satisfied that the equipment is running as it should, with no leaks or overflow, dechlorinate the water (if necessary), and add the salt. You now have a choice of either introducing Koi to your pond or, if it makes you more comfortable, adding "sacrificial" goldfish. The main problem with goldfish is that they multiply rapidly and you end up with a huge population you may not want. Purchase only a few fish to start. You are now ready to introduce your Koi to your pond. This is also the time to add the aerobic bacteria to help start up your bio-filter.

Your small population of fish will provide the waste needed to feed the bacteria so they will colonize and prosper. The manufacturer's instructions will tell you how often and for how long to add bacteria to the pond. However, you will only know if the bio-filter is functioning properly by testing the water daily for ammonia and nitrite levels. If your test shows any level of ammonia and/or nitrite, change about one-third of the pond volume to reduce the toxicity. Remember to add salt to replace the salt removed with the water. Even with perfect conditions, it will still take from four to six weeks in water temperatures above 77°F (25°C) to fully establish the bacteria colony. Expect to do fewer water changes as the colony establishes itself. You will likely experience an algae bloom in your pond during the first stages of getting your bio-filter into balance with the fish population. As the colony grows, you will see the water start to clear. Be patient. Getting a new bio-filter colonized is, beyond a doubt, the most difficult part of Koi keeping. On the other hand, once your bio-filter is up and functioning properly, it is very satisfying knowing that you have done it right. Your Koi will appreciate your efforts.

Continue to test the water on a weekly basis! Never become complacent about the quality of your pond's water. Without proper monitoring, today's success can become tomorrow's disaster.

KOI AND PLANTS

SHOWA

Plants and Koi live in harmony in well-cared-for ponds.

Forget everything you have heard about how impossible it is to successfully raise water plants in a Koi pond! It is possible and very simple.

If your Koi are well fed and their diet includes greens such as spinach and/or collard greens, they are much less likely to nibble on your plants. However, floating plants such as water lettuce and water hyacinths (and their roots, especially) are a favorite treat for Koi, no matter how well fed they may be.

Koi will start to eat floating plants almost as soon as they hit the water. Fortunately, this problem has been solved with the introduction of floating flora islands. The islands are made of a fine black-mesh netting on a round or square foam frame. You can either let them float or you can anchor them by a cord with a weight attached. This wonderful device allows the plants to benefit from the pond water, the pond to benefit from the plants, and the Koi to benefit from the shade the island(s) provides. Any roots that grow through the netting the Koi will eat and enjoy. As a result of this root pruning, your floating plants will grow vigorously.

Potted water plants present another problem. Koi love to root around in the dirt in the pots for whatever larvae, roots, and other treasures may be

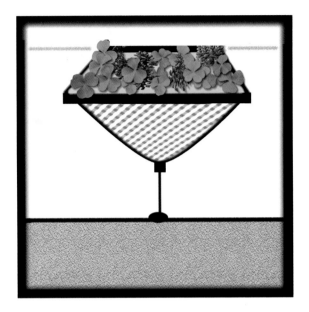 

FIGURES 19, 20 Square and round flora islands

hiding there. We found the solution about six years ago. Our new, larger pond was just completed, the Koi were safely acclimated to their new home, and it was time to place the plants in the pond. They were potted in a heavy soil. Even so, as soon as the pots came in contact with the water, some of the soil washed into the pond. Our nice, new, clean pond was instantly a cloudy mess. After much thought, and using my horticultural background as a guide, I saw the answer clearly: grow the water plants hydroponically. If you can grow a tomato in water rich in nutrients without soil, why not water plants? We removed the soil from the pots, placed each plant in the center of its pot, and replaced the soil with pieces of lava rock (flower rock) about the size of golf balls. We use plastic mesh baskets, which allow water to flow freely through them.

The plants flourished, to say the least. The Koi stayed out of the pots because they did not like the feel of the rough lava on their mouths. In addition, because lava rock is so porous and the water could flow freely through the plant baskets, we now had additional homes for the beneficial aerobic bacteria to colonize. Each plant basket became a miniature bio-filter.

Pebbles can also be used; however, Koi tend to remove them from the pots, eventually getting to the plant roots. Plus, pebbles do not have as much surface area as lava for aerobic bacteria. It is important to mention that we have never had an injury to a Koi as a result of using lava rock.

Oxygenating plants are submerged in the pond, pot and all. In this case a submerged plant protector is used to protect the plants from the Koi.

FIGURES 21, 22 Plant protectors

Some plants require soil: water lilies, rushes, and reeds, for example. Use a heavy soil with these, and top-dress with lava rock. Regarding lily pads, you may end up with damaged leaves no matter how well you feed your Koi. A floating plant protector will take care of this.

If you have or think you might have a predator problem, plants are a natural, decorative answer.

Place them on the shelf inside your pond. The Koi can swim around them and you will still have a barrier between the Koi and any animal that might come along.

Koi and plants belong together in nature and in our ponds. We simply need to provide our plants with some protection in our closed-system garden ponds.

CHAPTER NINE

SELECTING YOUR KOI

HI SHUSUI

The first step toward selecting healthy, beautiful Koi is finding a garden pond shop or garden center that is properly set up to sell Koi and all the related products.

Here are some things you should look for:

Clean Fish Display Tanks The tanks must have bio-filters to ensure the best water quality for the Koi. Ideally, each tank should have its own filtration system. If all the display tanks are on one system and a disease develops in one of the tanks, all the fish throughout the system will be exposed to the disease. The water should be clear and have no odor (unless the Koi have just been fed, in which case the water may have an ammonia odor briefly). The tanks and the area around them should be clean and orderly.

Quarantine Tanks New arrivals should be quarantined for at least two weeks before a dealer sells them, especially if the Koi are supplied by more than one source and include imported and domestic Koi. If your dealer is not quarantining Koi, you will need a facility of your own to keep the new Koi for at least two weeks before introducing them into your pond. Your quarantine tank or pond must be filtered and aerated. Koi should be made as comfortable in the quarantine tank as they will be in the pond they are going into (though the quarantine tank will be smaller than the pond) or they will become stressed and ill, defeating the purpose of quarantine. Always ask about the dealer's quarantine policy before making a purchase.

Information Regarding the Origin of the Koi Do not assume Koi are imported from Japan just because the sign reads "Japanese Koi." All Koi are Japanese Koi. Some are raised in Japan and are exported to other countries and some are raised in the country in which they are being sold. The latter should properly be referred to as domestic Japanese Koi.

The Koi being exported from Israel are often sold as Israeli Koi. There are no such Koi. They are simply Japanese Koi that have been raised in Israel. Koi imported from Japan are more expensive than domestically raised Koi due to the cost of shipping, losses, and the quality of the Koi, real or imagined. Without a doubt, Japanese Koi are of much better quality overall than Koi raised in other countries. The Japanese have been raising Koi for generations and they control the breeding stock. However, that does not guarantee that your dealer is importing Koi of high quality. Just because a Koi comes from Japan does not guarantee that it is a high-quality fish. Conversely, if the Koi your dealer is selling are raised locally, that does not automatically mean they are poor-quality fish. Over the last few years, the quality of Koi raised outside Japan has improved greatly. There is no reason to pay more for a Koi just because it is an import. Its value should be based on its quality and potential.

Clearly Defined Pricing Each tank should have a list of what it contains, *i.e.,* Koi, comets, shubunkins, and so on. Prices should be clearly marked and should be based on fish size and/or quality. If prices are based on size alone, it is possible to find "treasures" very reasonably.

Proper Nets for Catching Koi Your dealer should use and sell shallow, round nets with soft black netting. Deep nets slow the netting process because of the drag they create in the water. Chasing Koi around a tank or pond causes a great deal of stress not only for the fish being pursued, but the other fish as well. Also, deep nets bend the bodies of even the smaller fish, which can cause physical damage. Fish have difficulty seeing black netting and will often turn back into the net when trying to get away, making the catching process much easier. The dealer should keep all nets in a clean container, either dry or in medicated or heavily salted water. A net should never be propped against a wall where it might fall onto a dirty floor.

Oxygen Tank Oxygen must be added to each bag of fish that is to be transported. A dealer who does not provide oxygen does not know what he or she is doing or, even worse, does not care. Koi, or any fish that are caught and bagged, are automatically in a stressed state, which causes them to use up the oxygen in their water very rapidly. If oxygen has not been added to the bag they are in, they can easily become oxygen-deprived and die. This is especially true in hot weather. To lose Koi you have taken great care to select, because of negligence on the part of the dealer, is heartbreaking and unnecessary.

Guarantee Most dealers do not guarantee Koi, because they have no control over how you handle them once you leave their premises. A reasonable policy, if the dealer is doing his or her part, is to sell you healthy Koi.

Well Stocked and Well Organized Product Display Area A knowledgeable dealer will have products displayed in a way that makes it easy for you to find what you are looking for and discover new items. Good products have labels that describe the product and explain what it is used for and how to use it. Flashy, colorful labels will get your attention, but if they do not give specific information, they are of no use and are a waste of money. The label on water treatments, fish treatments, test kits, and the like should give you such information as how many gallons of water the container will treat or how many tests can be made. Food packages list ingredients. Ingredients are listed with the highest percentage contained in the food appearing first. Look for food packages that have different sizes of pellets. Some packages will even have a picture of the pellet size on the front of the wrapper. Attention to all these details will tell you that your dealer has done the research necessary to make the best possible products available to the Koi hobbyist.

If, however, products are in a state of disarray, you know immediately that the dealer does not take his garden pond department seriously, likely knows little or nothing about pond construction, Koi keeping, or bio-filtration, and will be of no help to you.

Knowledgeable Personnel This is an absolute must. Not only will you have someone to answer your questions and solve whatever problems you may have, you can also be confident that the Koi you are buying have been properly cared for and are in good health.

Now we can focus on the Koi and what to look for when selecting just the right one(s) for your pond. When I first started in the Koi hobby, I had no one to guide me. As a consequence, I am still living with my mistakes, or, more correctly, they are still living in my pond. My worst mistake was to buy a Koi because I felt sorry for it. I was sure it would not find a home unless I took it to my pond. To say it was not attractive would be kind. Adding to my mistake, I paid too much, because it was an imported Koi. Four years later she still lives happily, if unattractively, in my pond, and she is huge. So, now I not only have a really poor-quality Koi in my pond, I have a really poor-quality Koi that just keeps getting bigger. Learn from my mistake.

One of the reasons the first pond is always too small is the tendency to make mistakes at the beginning in selecting Koi. As you become more knowledgeable, you need more room to upgrade the quality of the Koi in your pond. No one I know is willing to destroy an old friend in the pond simply because it is not of good quality. Koi that survive our initial errors certainly deserve to live.

The first consideration when you are looking over a display tank of Koi is the overall appearance of each fish. As mentioned before, if the tanks are on a common filtration system carefully examine all the tanks for sick or weak-looking fish. Healthy, happy Koi will be swimming at all levels in the tanks (unless startled), have clear eyes, clear, unblemished skin, and full fins. White or red patches on the skin, fins that look as if they are rotting away, bulging eyes, open sores, big heads on sunken bodies, and gasping for air at the surface are all warning signs of fish that are neglected and sick. If the Koi you select has any of these symptoms or has been exposed to them, you must not take it home or you will infect your entire pond. Once you have determined that the Koi are healthy, you can concentrate on their quality.

Before going any further, I would like to say that if you think a Koi is beautiful, it is. Have confidence in your choices. If the Koi you select give you pleasure, that is all that matters.

We had the opportunity to visit a Koi farm with our club a few years ago, and we were given the opportunity to buy Koi after the tour. Each of us was given a number, and we waited our turn before entering the display area. In theory, this meant that the best Koi would be purchased by those who saw them first. When it was my turn to enter, one of the Koi immediately caught my eye. However, since many of the members (who were much more experienced than I) had already made purchases, I could not imagine why, if the Koi I was interested in was as good as I thought, it had it not been purchased. My problem was not whether I wanted the Koi or not; I certainly did. My problem was being afraid of making a poor choice in the presence of my peers. In the end, I realized how ridiculous I was being and I purchased the treasured Koi that had caught my eye. As my Koi was being bagged for transport, two farm employees congratulated me on my choice. They had expected that Koi to be one of the first to sell. What really made me feel more confident about my choice, however, was a conversation I had during lunch. I was again congratulated on my choice by the gentleman sitting next to me He was the same person who had been standing next to me in the display area and had unknowingly almost intimidated me to the point of passing on the purchase. As it turned out, he was hoping I would make another choice because he wanted "my" Koi. Choose your Koi by your own standards of beauty. After all, beauty is in the eye of the beholder. Certainly, there are judging standards for a reason, but not all of us aspire to show our Koi. There are many, many lovely Koi that will never win a prize!

We all have our favorite varieties. I am very partial to the robed *(koromo)* Koi. However, too much of a good thing does not make a very interesting pond. Be sure your selections add new interest and color to your pond.

Kohaku, showa, sanke, ogon, asagi and *shusui* are basic varieties. These are all very popular among collectors and are generally fairly easy to find. Although they do not show up very well in a pond, black Koi are prized by many collectors. It is fun to see what the original Koi looked like and compare it to how they have developed over the centuries.

Take your time looking over all the Koi that are displayed. Small Koi take more time to select. There are usually many to choose from and their good points and bad are not as apparent as they are on the larger fish. Remember, the better the color and the sharper the pattern on a small fish, the more likely it is to lose quality than it is to improve with maturity. Remember the old Japanese saying, "It is a fool who buys a three-inch Koi and it is a fool who sells one." The red on a young Koi should be orange/red. The white moves upward from the bel-

Koi sales pond in England

Aka-Bekko

the pattern would look if all the gray areas were black. The head should not be speckled. Excellent color, balanced pattern with a sharp edge (*kiwa*), and a well-shaped body and head are all features you should look for when buying mature Koi. Keep in mind that a Koi possessing all these qualities is a show-quality fish and not likely to be found in your local shop unless your dealer is selling very, very expensive Koi.

Except for obvious defects, such as a crooked spine or mouth, do not concentrate on the flaws. Instead, consider all the good points of the Koi. Most important is that the Koi is healthy, you like it, and it will add color and beauty to your pond.

After you have made your selection and the Koi has been netted and bagged, your dealer should hold up the bag and examine your Koi thoroughly. If this is not done, insist on doing it yourself before completing the purchase.

ly with growth, which can change the pattern for the better or the worse. *The sumi* (black) may be very black in some areas and dark gray like a shadow in others. The gray under the skin is the black that will come to the surface as the Koi matures, which will change the pattern considerably. Visualize how

INTRODUCING NEW KOI TO YOUR POND

GINRIN SHOWA

You have selected healthy Koi, and they have been inspected and bagged properly. Now it is up to you to safely introduce your new friends to their new pond. Any time Koi are taken from one environment and placed in another, the proper steps must be followed to acclimate them to the temperature and pH of their new home. Floating the plastic bag in your pond is not enough. Here is the proper acclimating procedure to follow to ensure their survival.

1. Place the plastic bag containing the Koi in your pond or quarantine tank. Open the bag and secure it to the side.

2. To establish how much of a difference in pH levels you need to adjust your fish to, test the pH level in the plastic bag and the pH in your pond.

3. Assuming you have a gallon or less of water in the bag, take out approximately two cups (0.5 l) of water and throw it away. Do not put the water from the bag into your pond or quarantine tank. Stressed fish create a great deal of waste material.

4. The rule is, take an equal amount of water out of the bag and replace it with an equal amount from the new pond or quarantine tank.

5. Repeat this procedure every 15 minutes for an hour.

6. Test the pH level of the water in the bag.

7. Test the temperature of the water in the bag and the water the Koi are going into. Most people can put one hand in the bag and the other in the pond and judge how close the temperatures are.

8. If the pH levels are the same and the water temperatures are the same or very close, you are ready to release your new Koi.

9. Make sure your hands are clean and free of any oils or lotions. Gently reach into the bag and get a firm but gentle hold on the Koi. Lift the Koi out of the bag and place it in its new home. Generally, holding the head and upper body quiets the fish. Larger Koi will require two hands, so have another person hold the bag. Position the bag over the water at all times during the releasing process, so that if the Koi gets away from you it will fall into the pond and not onto a hard surface. However, if this should happen, do not panic. Make sure your hands are wet (the Koi's protective slime coat will come off on dry hands), place one hand over the eyes and head, the other hand over the back end of the fish, and pick it up as gently but firmly as possible.

10. Throw away the dirty water from the bag. Pour it on the grass or water the nearest plant with it. It is great fertilizer.

If you are just getting started and your Koi are the first fish in your pond, give them a day or two to settle down before feeding them. Feed sparingly until they adjust to their new surroundings. If other fish are already in the pond, the newcomers will follow the lead of the veteran residents and will settle in more quickly.

You have done everything right, so sit back and enjoy your new Koi.

WATER QUALITY

SHIRO BEKKO

WATER QUALITY LIMITS FOR A SUCCESSFUL POND

Listed below are the required parameters for a healthy Koi pond, along with suggested testing schedules and steps to correct any harmful levels. Test kits are available.

ppm = parts per million

pH 6.8 to 8.2

Alkalinity 50 to 100 ppm

Hardness (calcium and magnesium) 50 to 150 ppm

Dissolved oxygen (O_2) more than 7 ppm

Dissolved carbon dioxide (CO_2) less than 5 ppm

Free ammonia (NH_3) less than 0.005 ppm

Total ammonia ($NH + NH_4$) less than 0.05 ppm

Nitrite (NO_2) less than 0.05 ppm

Dissolved organic carbon (DOC) very little (colors water yellow and creates foam; stresses Koi).

pH: Test twice a week, at dawn and dusk. Biological filters add acidity to a pond.

Alkalinity and Hardness: This needs to be tested only two or three times a year. Add baking soda (sodium bicarbonate: $NaHCO_3$) to increase alkalinity without adding hardness. This will stabilize the pH around 7.8. Never use swimming pool chemicals to lower the pH. The alkalinity (as distinct from pH) serves to buffer the pond against a change in pH. If you try to lower the pH by adding something acidic, the pH will not drop until the alkalinity is used up; therefore, when you add acidity with no result and then add just a little bit more, the pH will drop out of sight, resulting in damage to the Koi. Also, without buffering, plants and/or algae can cause high pH in the afternoon and low pH at night (see below). There are products available that are specifically for increasing and decreasing pH in ponds. Used exactly as directed, they will adjust your pH safely.

Oxygen: Test weekly. Test more often during extremely hot weather. You cannot not have too much oxygen in your pond.

Carbon Dioxide: There should be no reason to test for CO_2 unless a problem arises. Good aeration will drive off excess carbon dioxide.

Ammonia and Nitrite: There should never be ammonia or nitrite in the pond in measurable amounts. Pond water should always test zero. If it does not, something is wrong with the filtering system.

Interaction of Water-Quality Variables: All water chemistry factors are related to each other. Changing one can change several others.

The following chart shows how these factors are influenced by everyday activities.

Activity	pH	NH_4	O_2	CO_2	DOC	Turbidity
Population Level	Down	Up	Down	Up	Up	Up
Mechanical Filter	Up	Down	Up	—	Down	Down
Foam Fractionator	Up	Down	Up	Down	Down	Down
Biological Filter	Down	Down	Down	Down	Up	Up
Plants/Algae Day	Up	Down	Up	Down	Up	Up
Plants/Algae Night	Down	Up	Down	Up	Up	Up

Beware of compound stress effects. Several small factors can combine to produce disastrous results.

Population Levels: A very important factor. A good rule to follow is to have no more than one inch of Koi per square foot of pond surface area (or 28 cm per sq m), assuming there is a good bio-filter and good aeration. This demonstrates how a properly stocked pond can become a vastly over-crowded pond in just a year or two as your Koi grow, causing water-quality problems.

Overcrowding: Overcrowding reduces oxygen levels and increases the ammonia and nitrite load on the bio-filter.

Aeration: Be sure your pond is well aerated at all times. When oxygen levels are low, the largest Koi die first. If you see this happening in your pond, check oxygen levels immediately.

Winter Ice: Keeping a hole in the ice allows toxic gases, such as hydrogen sulfide, to escape.

Dissolved Organic Carbons (DOC): This can be removed with a foam fractionator.

A Koi pond in Virginia

CHAPTER TWELVE

WHAT EXACTLY IS pH?

BUTTERFLY KOI

According to Webster's New Collegiate Dictionary, pH is the negative logarithm of the effective hydrogen-ion concentration or hydrogen-ion activity, in gram equivalents per liter, used in expressing both acidity and alkalinity on a scale whose values run from 0 to 14, with 7 representing neutrality. Numbers less than 7 increase acidity and numbers more than 7 increase alkalinity.

Logarithmic means that a pH of 5.0 is 10 times more acidic than 6.0 and 100 times more acidic than 7.0. Conversely, a pH of 9.0 is 10 times more alkaline than 8.0 and 100 times more alkaline than 7.0

For pond owners: The factors that make one source of water more acidic than another are fish solid waste (nitrite), the water source, the bio-filter, and rotting food and vegetation. Water plants, bog plants, and algae increase the acidity by replacing the calcium, manganese, and potassium they take in with hydrogen and aluminum ions. Fish liquid waste (ammonia) also affects water acidity when ammonium nitrogen (NH_4^+) is converted into nitrite nitrogen (NH_3, the form of nitrogen most readily utilized by plants), releasing hydrogen ions into the water, increasing its acidity.

When fish turn and rub themselves on the sides and bottom of the pond it is called "flashing" and can be caused by parasites or a substantial change in the pH. If your Koi only flash at a particular time of the day, test for sudden pH changes as a normal routine at dawn and dusk.

POND
MAINTENANCE

TAISHO SANKE
BRED IN TAIWAN

As time goes by and the pond is testing beautifully, the tendency is to become complacent and neglect to take water tests as often as necessary. This is especially true if the pond water is *gin*, clear, and the Koi are cruising around the pond without any signs of discomfort and are eating voraciously. However, sudden changes in temperature, anaerobic bacteria growth, filter channeling, and rainfall are factors that can quickly change pristine conditions to deadly ones. Only by testing the water on a regular basis will you have the information you need to be in control of the water quality in your pond.

Checking the water temperature, so you know how many times a day to feed and how much protein to feed, will keep your Koi and your bio-filter in top condition. Always remember that what goes in and out of your Koi directly effects the bio-filter. Check your bio-filter often and gently rinse off any heavy waste material. Keep your skimmer(s) clear of debris.

Clean out any debris on the bottom of the pond. Remove dead or dying plant material. Sticks and leaves that cannot be vacuumed out can be removed with a small net designed for this purpose. Do not use your good Koi net for cleaning.

There are a variety of ways to remove dirt from the bottom of your pond. If you have a bottom drain, most of the waste will travel down the natural slope provided when the drain was installed. The only help needed to get rid of the unwanted material on the bottom is an occasional push with a brush on a long handle to direct the debris toward the drain while it is open. The normal path of the bottom drain is to the settlement chamber or to the bio-filter, but with properly fitted valves you can shut off that path, open another, and direct the flow to a garden, sump, or other drain area.

Without a bottom drain you will need a pond vacuum, which is a device powered by a garden hose or connected to a pump. The debris goes into a mesh bag or is discharged through a hose to your drainage area. This makes a perfect fertilizer for your garden.

An hour or less each weekend should keep your pond in top condition with very little work.

A Koi pond in England

71

SPRING CLEANUP

DOITSU SANKE

This is without a doubt our favorite pond project. Every spring, we pick the first warm, clear day when the water is still cool. Koi are not active in cool water, which makes them easier to catch. The object is to get the pond clean and ready for the spring season while causing as little stress as possible to the Koi. This is a wet, messy job, so wear old clothes and comfortable shoes that you don't mind getting wet and dirty.

So where is the fun in all this? For us it is the opportunity to see our Koi up close after the long winter. We can measure, examine, and even weigh them. Each Koi is handled gently and quickly released into the holding tank after being inspected for wounds, disease, or parasites. If there are any problems, we take care of them in the early stages, before the pond water warms up and the problem(s) escalate.

You will need some type of container to put your Koi in while you are cleaning the pond. Do not use deep, narrow trash cans. Your Koi will not have enough room and will become stressed. If you must clean your pond on a hot day, putting your Koi in such a container will more than likely lead to disaster. A children's plastic wading pool, a livestock watering tank, or, if you are fortunate enough to have one, a portable Koi show tank are much better choices. Whatever you use, be sure it is clean!

Fill your holding tank with water from the pond. This is the water your Koi are used to. If you have an air pump, aerate the tank. Additional oxygen is always a good idea. Cover the tank with netting and secure every inch of it. It is amazing how Koi can jump through the smallest spaces when they are excited. If one of your Koi does jump, wet your hands before attempting to pick it up. Your best approach is to place one hand over the head and eyes and gently but firmly pick up the Koi when you are sure you have it under control.

Position the tank in a shaded area away from the work area but close enough so you can easily see if your Koi start to have a problem (gasping at the top, for example, or jumping out). Neither situation should arise unless you have crowded them or covered them incorrectly, *e.g.*, with plastic.

Now, lower the water in your pond so the Koi are easier to catch. Do not lower the water to the point where the backs of the Koi are out of the water or so low that they have to swim on their sides. Your Koi will panic under either of these conditions. Unless your pond is very small, you need to get into the pond to catch the fish. Ideally, you have purchased a round, shallow Koi net. The moment of truth has arrived, and it is time to pit man (or woman) against Koi. Don't be in a hurry; that is when accidents happen and fish get hurt. Take your time! Pick out the fish you want to catch and concentrate on only that one until you have it in your net. Pursue the Koi slowly. Do not splash and thrash around the pond. Once caught, the Koi should be examined while it is still in the net. Hold the net about halfway in the water. Place one hand over the head and eyes, and the Koi should relax a little, making it easier for you to turn it over for a close examination of the entire body. This operation really requires two people. In our case, one of us catches the Koi and brings it over to the side of the pond; we both examine it, and then the other one of us takes the Koi, net and all, and releases it gently into the holding tank.

After the last Koi has been transferred and we are

sure they cannot escape, we empty the pond all the way down and start scrubbing the sides and bottom with clean water. Since our pond was built before we knew about bottom drains, we pump the dirty water out with a sump pump. Next, we give our bio-filter a good rinse. Then, if we are satisfied that the winter dirt has been removed, we hook up the UV sterilizer, the waterfall, and the fountain, and we start filling the pond.

While your pond is filling, add salt (rock salt is fine as long as it is clean and contains no additives) at a rate of 1/2 pound (225 grams) per 100 gallons (380 liters). Whatever salt you use, be sure it does not contain iodine or additives. If your water contains chlorine or chloramines, add a dechlorinator. A good dechlorinator also removes toxic heavy metals from non-chlorinated or well water. You cannot reintroduce your Koi or add the bacteria until all the chlorine is removed. Chlorine kills fish, plants, and beneficial bacteria as well as disease-causing bacteria. Test kits are available and worth purchasing. Testing the pond water will tell you if you have been successful in removing all the chlorine or if you need to add more of the dechlorinator. Once that is done, you may add a bacterial start-up product so your bio-filter will be fully func-

tional in the shortest possible time. Now you can safely reintroduce your Koi to the pond.

When the pond is full, turn on your bio-filter, waterfall, or other feature. Your pond is now clean, dechlorinated, salted, and ready to receive the Koi, but your Koi are not ready. You must now acclimate them to their new environment before putting them back into the pond, using the same method you use when you bring home a new Koi, only on a larger scale. Take a bucket of water out of the holding tank (two, if the tank is over 150 gallons/570 liters) and empty it into the nearest flower bed. Take the same amount of water from the pond and pour it into the holding tank. Repeat every 15 or 20 minutes for at least an hour. Then test the pH and temperature of the holding tank and the pond. When they test the same or very close, you can release your Koi into the pond gently, one at a time. Again, take your time! Accidents happen when people are tired or in too much of a hurry.

Now comes the best part. Your pond is clean. Your bio-filter, UV sterilizer, waterfall, and fountain(s) are up and running, and your Koi are safely swimming in a nice, clean pond. All that is left for you to do now is to sit back and enjoy!

PREPARING YOUR POND FOR WINTER

YAMATANISHIKI

Koi withstand cold temperatures very well, providing their environment is as clean and free of toxins as it was during warmer weather. Freezing cold weather presents an additional problem. If your pond freezes over, the toxic gases given off by the breakdown of any vegetation or waste that might be present cannot escape into the air and are trapped under the ice. Koi are much more likely to die of asphyxiation than from the cold. Knowing this, we must make every effort to provide an escape for these gases. Running your waterfall to keep water moving, which in turn would keep a hole in the ice, sounds like a good solution, but it isn't. The water in your waterfall comes from the warmest water in your pond. If you take that water, run it up to the waterfall and out into the freezing air, you are sending the water back to the pond colder than when it left. Each time the water cycles from the pond to the waterfall and back, the pond gets colder.

Never assume that because you are not feeding your Koi they are not giving off waste products. During the winter Koi are likely to feed occasionally on the algae around the sides of your pond. The ammonia and nitrites they eliminate may be minimal, but they can accumulate to threatening levels.

Now that we have addressed the problems, let us address the solutions. We recommend the following winterizing procedures:

1. Turn off your waterfall and by-pass the water directly to the pond.

2. Keep your bio-filter running. If your filter is not sheltered, insulate it with straw, leaves, mulch, whatever you have available to keep it from freezing.

3. If you have a small pond, a livestock water tank de-icer will keep a hole in the ice. You do not need to heat the entire pond. If you have a large pond, take a small pump, put an extension on the discharge and set it on your plant shelf. The pump will bubble the water, which will keep a hole in the ice and aerate the water as well. By placing the pump on the shelf rather than on the bottom of the pond, you will not destratify the water and stir up unwanted particulate matter. We use our fountain pump.

4. Turn off your UV sterilizer, drain it, clean with bleach, rinse well, and store indoors.

5. Turn off your fountain(s), clean and store indoors.

6. Lower the level of your pond by a few inches to allow for the winter rain and snow accumulation.

7. Keep all submersible pumps stored in water to keep their seals from drying out.

8. Cover your pond with a pond cover to prevent leaves and debris from accumulating in your pond. Remember, leaves break down and create toxic gases. If possible, buy a commercially made pond cover. Making one yourself out of bird netting or deer netting can prove fatal to your Koi. That type of netting sags down into the water under the weight of the leaves and your Koi can become trapped in it.

9. Remove any debris that is present in your pond.

If you must shut off your bio-filter, clean it thoroughly before storing it for the winter. An inactive bio-filter is filled with dead matter. Pumping this dead debris into your pond when you start up in the spring would definitely not get your pond off to the proper start for the season.

Your Koi should get through the winter just fine if you have taken the above steps and prepared them for the cold weather with the proper feeding regimen.

Kujaku

SPAWNINGS

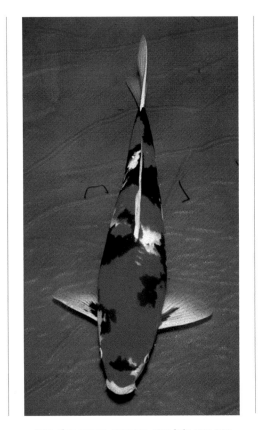

Hi Showa Bred in Taiwan

Most beginning hobbyists get all excited about the possibility of their Koi spawning and producing lots of beautiful little Koi. Not likely. True, your Koi will no doubt eventually spawn, but it is very unlikely that they will produce any beautiful offspring.

We are not going to get very technical here, but suffice it to say that generations of Japanese have been breeding generations of Koi from the same bloodlines. They know exactly what a small Koi should look like from their line(s) and if it will grow into a Koi worth keeping. Knowing that, what possible chance do any of us have to produce one, let alone many, Koi of reasonable quality? Out of one spawn with proven breeders, the Japanese growers will ultimately cull all but 300 to 600 Koi. Only those Koi will be sold. The rest become food for the remaining stock. Don't get upset. They are very environmentally correct in what they are doing. The fact that a female can produce 100,000 eggs tells us that the eggs are part of the food chain. On commercial Koi farms, they lay out spawning mats for the females and gather up the mats after the spawn. Thus, the food chain has been deprived of critical protein. Putting the protein back into the food chain is the responsible thing to do.

Assuming you have a healthy pond and healthy Koi, your Koi will eventually spawn when they reach sexual maturity. We did not have a spawn in our pond until our Koi were at least 12 inches long. The size of a sexually mature Koi seems to vary, however. At the present time two of our younger 9-inch females are definitely heavy with eggs. Every time our Koi have spawned it has been triggered by a temperature change from cool to warm. Although the books told us that Koi spawn in the early morning, ours have always spawned in the afternoon.

Ki Goi bred in Taiwan

Taisho Sanke bred in Taiwan

Spawning is an interesting and somewhat violent event to watch. The males swim head-first into the side of the female, driving her into plants or rocks where she can deposit her eggs. The males then fertilize the eggs by releasing their milt. When that female has released all of her eggs, the males proceed to drive another female, until all of the egg-heavy females have deposited their eggs.

If the females are driven into rocks they become injured, sometimes critically. There is an easy solution to this problem as long as you are there when the spawning begins. Gather ferns or branches from any bush that produces soft stems and multiple leaves. Never use vegetation that has been sprayed with an insecticide. Make bundles and throw them into the pond. The males will then drive the female into the bundles and she can deposit her eggs unharmed. This will also give you control over the eggs and you can do with them what you wish. Since we average about four or five large females to a spawning, we gather up the bundles and throw them away.

During the process of the spawning, a dangerous amount of ammonia is released into the pond. The more Koi involved, the higher the level of ammonia. When the spawning activity has stopped, test for ammonia immediately and start changing the water. Run water in and pump water out at the same time so the temperature of the water changes gradually and the toxicity of the ammonia is diluted immediately. Keep testing until your ammonia level is zero.

The last time our Koi spawned, even with the help of the bundles of fern, there were still eggs everywhere in the pond. The Koi gorged on the eggs for three days. We discontinued feeding.

Although you have removed most of the eggs and changed almost all of the water in your pond, you will more than likely find baby Koi swimming around in a month or two. Enjoy!

They are yours, and you don't care if you are the only one who thinks they are beautiful.

CHAPTER SEVENTEEN

PROBLEMS
AND SUGGESTED
SOLUTIONS

SANDAN KOHAKU

ACIDITY/ALKALINITY: Adding 1 ounce of sodium bicarbonate (NAH-CO₃) per 100 gallons of water will assist in neutralizing the pH without adding hardness. Sodium bicarbonate brings up the acidic level and conversely brings down the alkalinity to a neutral level.

Hardness: Salt is a natural softener, but use only non-iodized salt for your pond. The effect in your pond is quite the same as from the salt used in home water conditioners. The salt will only dissolve until a salinity level is reached; then no more will dissolve until the level is reduced by the addition of more water. For Koi ponds, the softening is only part of the benefit. It also assists in osmo-regulation, the build-up of a good slime coat, and the control of some parasites, and, if used as recommended, it will not harm water plants.

Dissolved Oxygen (DO): Waterfalls, spillways, fountains, air stones, venturis, and oxygenating plants provide oxygen. The simple task of building a good waterfall or spillway will aerate the water and enhance the audible pleasure of your pond.

Carbon Dioxide (CO₂): Carbon dioxide is a heavy, colorless gas that is formed by the decomposition of organic substances. It is absorbed from the air by plants in photosynthesis. Simple aeration will assist in the removal.

Ammonia: Effective bio-filtration, and aeration. Not only will the ammonia be converted by the aerobic bacteria in the bio-filter, but some will be disbursed through good aeration.

Nitrite: Effective bio-filtration and plants are the most effective way to rid your pond of nitrite.

Dissolved Organic Carbon (DOC): A protein skimmer (foam fractionator), which may or may not be necessary at all times, depending on the quality of your bio-filter and other influences.

Disease Prevention: Water quality! Diet! Vitamin C, trace minerals, selenium for immune-system collagen found in Swiss chard. Salt in the pond water, efficient bio-filtration system, good aeration, plenty of water movement and water changes to replace spent electrolytes. Quarantine all new arrivals.

Temperature Extremes: Winter: keep a hole in the ice to allow toxic gases to escape. Summer: water changes to cool down the pond water.

Overcrowding: Larger bio-filter and/or larger pond; remove some of your Koi.

Algae: Efficient bio-filter, plus an ultraviolet sterilizer. Filtered sun.

Pollen: Water cleans air; therefore, your pond has two or three times as much pollen as your car or picnic table. A surface skimmer helps.

Crustaceans: Soak new plants in a solution of 12 drops of vinegar per quart of water for one minute before introducing them into your pond.

Phosphate: Run water through an activated carbon filter that is attached to your garden hose before the water enters the pond. Remember, carbon absorbs. When it reaches saturation it must be recharged or replaced.

SPECIFIC DISEASES

Symptoms	Possible Diagnosis	Action	Treatment
Cottony puffs	Fungus	Treat	Fungus-Ease
Darkens; hides on pond bottom	Skin parasites	Treat	Trichloracide
	Internal parasites		Medicated food to all fish 10 days
Eyes protrude	Bacterial infection		Medicated food to all fish 10 days
Fading colors	pH	Test	Change water
	Chemicals		Change water
	Medication		Change water
	Lawn fertilizer		Change water
	Stale food		New food
	Poor food		Change food
Fecal matter does not detach	Bacteria		Medicated food to all fish 10 days
	Flagellates		Medicated food to all fish 10 days
Fins edged in white, deteriorate	Bacterial fin rot	Treat	Furoplex & Wound-Ease
Fins fray & become whitish	pH too high or too low	Test	Adjust pH; see Chapter 12
Folded fins & scraped bodies	Parasites	Treat	Trichloricide & Wound-Ease
Gills gray	Bacterial gill disease	Treat	B.G.D.X.

Symptoms	Possible Diagnosis	Action	Treatment
Mouth wounds	Eating from hard objects	Treat	Wound-Ease
Moves slowly; swims near surface	Ammonia poisoning	Test	Change water; see Chapter 4
	Nitrite poisoning	Test	Change water & clean & reseed filter
Jumps around & colors fade	Toxin in water		Change water
Sandlike white spots	Ich (a parasite) Ichthyophthiris	Treat	Ich-Ease
Scrape or puncture	Rocks or object in pond	Treat	Furoplex to prevent secondary infection
	Predator		Wound-Ease to heal wound
Small white dots on gills	Gill crustations	Treat	Trichloricide & Wound-Ease
Stringlike worms attached to fish	Anchor worm (a parasite) (Lernae)	Treat	Trichloricide & Wound-Ease
Swims normally; breathes heavily	High water temperature	Test	Change water
	Oxygen deficiency	Test	Aerate/change water
	Excess carbon dioxide		Clean pond & filter
Transparent disks causing red wounds	Carp louse	Treat	Trichloricide & Wound-Ease
Whitish solid waxy lumps	Carp pox		Disappears as water warms; generally not harmful
Worms on gills	Gill flukes	Treat	Trichloride & Wound-Ease

NOTE: The suggested treatments are the ones we have found to be the most effective. Before treating your pond, always read the label on the medication for information regarding the effect it may have on your bio-filter.

CHAPTER EIGHTEEN

KOI CLASSIFICATIONS

ORENJI HARIWAKE

Classification	Variety	Color and Description
AI GOROMO	9	White body with red patterns and blue robe
AI SHOWA	9	Indigo dark blue robe
AKA BEKKO	2	Red body with black patterns
AKA HAJIRO	5	Red body with white fins
AKA MUJI	5	Plain red; not considered desirable
AKA SANKE	1	Black spotlike patterns on red patterns continuous from head to beginning of tail
AKA MATSUBA	5	Red body with black markings in center of the scales
AKAME KI GOI	5	Bright yellow Koi with red eyes
ASAGI SANKE	11	Pale blue back, red head and sides
ASAGI SUMINAGASHI	11	Black body with scales outlined in white
BENI GOI	5	Very deep red, non-metallic
BENI KUJAKU	3	Red, dominating five-color *Kujaku*
BOKE SHOWA	10	Faded *Showa*
BUDO SANKE OR SANSHOKU	11	Black under red scales, appearing purple
CHA GOI	5	Single brownish green-colored, non-metallic, with somewhat reticulated scales
DOITSU AKA-MATSUBA	5	Red body with large dark *Doitsu* scales

Classification	*Variety*	*Color and Description*
DOITSU KI-MATSUBA	5	Large yellow *Doitsu* scales, pinecone pattern
DOITSU KUJAKU	3	Red and gold on platinum with dark pinecone *Doitsu* scales
DOITSU HARIWAKE-PLATINUM	6	Platinum body with clear platinum *Doitsu* scales
DOITSU SHIRO-MATSUBA	5	White body, with black only on *Doitsu* scales
FUJI OGON	6	Any *Ogon* with a metallic head
FUJI SANKE	11	*Sanke* with metallic luster on the head
GIN BEKKO	3	Platinum body with black markings
GINBO	6	Silver metallic *Ogon*
GIN KABUTO	6	Silver pattern covering most of the dorsal
GIN MATSUBA	6	White body with pinecone scale pattern
GINRIN SANKE	7	Silver-scaled *Sanke*
GINRIN-SHIRO MUJI	4	Solid white with silver scales
GINRIN SHOWA	7	Silver-scaled *Showa*
GINRIN TANSHO	7	Silver scales on a *Kohaku*, *Showa*, or *Sanke* with a red spot pattern on the head only
GINRIN UTSURI	7	Silver *Utsuri*
GIN SHIRO	4	Metallic silver *Utsuri*

Classification	Variety	Color and Description
GIN SHOWA	4	Metallic silver *Showa*
GIN SUI	3	Metallic-blue *Shusui* (very little or no red)
GIN UTSURI	4	Black with silver metallic scales
GOSHIKI	5	Five colors: white, red, black, blue, and dark blue
GOSHIKI SHUSUI	5	*Doitsu*, non-metallic, five colors
GOTEN-ZAKURA	8	A *Kohaku* with cherry blossom pattern that looks like bunches of grapes
HAGESHIRO	5	Black with white on cheeks and nose
HAJIRO	5	Black with white tips on the fins, "Crow"
HANA SHUSUI	1	*Doitsu* scales, white head, blue and red between belly and lateral lines and between lateral lines and dorsal, "Flowery *Shusui*"
HARIWAKE MATSUBA	3	Metallic platinum body with gold patches and pinecone scales
HARIWAKE OGON	6	Platinum body with metallic gold patterns
HI ASAGI	1	The red on the belly extends above the lateral line, sometimes to the dorsal fin.
HI BOTAN	5	*Taisho Sanshoku* with large blotches of black (*sumi*) on the dorsal area
HI KAGE UTSURI	13	Red, with black shadow reflection

Classification	Variety	Color and Description
HI NO MARU	12	*Tancho*, "a crimson disk on white ground"
HI SHUSUI	1	Red from belly to dorsal
HI SHOWA	10	Red dominating over black and white *Showa*
HI UTSURI	4	Black with accents of intense scarlet red
KAGE GIN SHIRU	5	Silver body with very faint black and red patterns under the skin
KAGE KAWARI MONO	5	Black scale edgings on white, red or yellow
KAGE HI UTSURI	13	Black scale edgings on red
KAGE KI UTSURI	13	Black scale edgings on yellow
KAGE SHIRO UTSURI	13	Black scale edgings on white
KAGE SHOWA	10	White scales have thin black lines around the edge.
KAKU TAN	12	Rectangular-patterned *Tancho*
KARASU GOI	5	All-black body
KAWARI MONO	5	Novelty or rare class, non-metallic
KI BEKKO	2	Yellow-colored body with black patterns
KI GOI	5	Yellow non-metallic
KI MATSUBA	5	Yellow body with pinecone scales

Classification	Variety	Color and Description
KIKUSUI	3	Metallic platinum *Doitsu* with brilliant orange or gold along the lateral line, "Chrysanthemum Water"
KINDAI SHOWA	10	White dominating over red and black
KINBO	6	Metallic gold *Ogon* (*Aka Kin-Kabuto*)
KINGINRIN KOHAKU	3	Gold and silver diamond-scale *Kohaku*
KIN HI UTSURI	4	Metallic red *Utsuri*
KIN KI UTSURI	4	Metallic yellow *Utsuri*
KIN OGON	6	Solid-gold *Ogon*
KINRIN AKA MUJI	6	Solid orange with metallic gold scales
KINRIN BEKKO	7	Metallic gold-scaled *Bekko*
KINRIN SHOWA	7	Metallic gold-scaled *Showa*
KINRIN UTSURI	7	Metallic gold-scaled *Utsuri*
KINSUI	7	Metallic, predominantly red, *Shusui*
KI UTSURI	4	Black with accents of yellow
KOROMO SHOWA	9	*Showa* whose red has a bluish cast
KUJAKU	3	Red and gold on platinum with dark pinecone scales
KUMONRYU	5	Black and white *Doitsu*

KOI CLASSIFICATIONS

Classification	Variety	Color and Description
KONJO ASAGI	1	Very dark, almost black, *Asagi*
MATSUBA OGON	5	Single color with pinecone pattern
MATSUBA KAWARI	3	Red, yellow or white with black pinecone scales. Metallic gold, silver, yellow, or red in body and pinecone scales in the dorsal
MIDORIGOI	5	Green *Doitsu* carp variation of the *Shusui*
MIZU ASAGI	1	Very light-patterned *Asagi*
MUJI KAWARI MONO	5	Non-metallic with one solid color
NARUMI ASAGI	1	Light blue-patterned *Asagi*
NEZU OGON	3	Solid-silver metallic
ORENJI HAREWAKE	3	Platinum body with metallic orange patterns
ORENJI OGON	3	Metallic orange
PLATINUM KOHAKU	3	Metallic platinum *Kohaku*
SANKURA OGON	3	Metallic platinum with cherry-like patterns
SANSHOKU SANKE	11	Non-metallic tricolor of white, red, and black, the black less dominant than on the *Showa*
SHINZO TANCHO	12	Pattern is a heart-shaped crest.
SHIRO BEKKO	2	White body with black spots

Classification	Variety	Color and Description
SHIRO UTSURI	13	Black body with white patterns
SHO CHIKU BAI	3	Metallic *Ai-Gromo*
SHOWA (SANSHOKU)	10	Black, red and white with black dominating and on the head
SHUSUI	1	Red and blue *Doitsu*, "Autumn Water" or "Autumn Sky." Red may run parallel on the dorsal, forming a red striped pattern.
SUMI GOROMO	9	Black robe on red pattern
TAISHO SANKE	11	White with black on the body and single red pattern on the head
TAKI SANKE	1	Blue body separated from red sides with a white line on the lateral
TANCHO KOHAKU	8	White body with red pattern on the head only
TANCHO SANKE	11	White body, black patterns, red only on the head
TAKI ASAGI	1	Red and blue with pinecone pattern
TORA OGON	3	Metallic gold with black patterns on dorsal
TSUBAKI SANKE	11	A large *Sanke* with a black pattern from head to dorsal area
UTSURI MONO	13	Black with white, red or yellow (reflection class)

Classification	Variety	Color and Description
YAMABUKI-HAREWAKE	3	Platinum body with metallic patterns
YAMABUKI OGON	6	Bright yellow with gold metallic scales
YAMATO NISHIKI	6	*Taisho Sanke* with high metallic luster
YOTSU-SHIRO	5	*Karasu* with white on head, fins and tail
ZUIUN	5	A *Midorigoi* variation with a light purple dorsal, shading to light blue as it reaches the belly

Variety	Basic Description
1. ASAGI AND SHUSUI	Pale blue-back, orange/red belly. *Asagi* is scaled; *Shusui* is *Doitsu*.
2. BEKKO	White, red or yellow base. Black pattern
3. HIKARI-MOYOMONO	Shiny-patterned. All metallic with the exception of *Ogon, Showa,* and *Utsuri*
4. HIKARI-UTSURIMONO	Metallic *Utsurimono* (see 13) and metallic *Showa* (see 10)
5. KAWARIMONO	Unusual ones. Non-classified varieties. Non-metallic
6. HIKARI-MUJIMONO	One metallic color
7. KINGINRIN	Koi with rows of metallic silver scales on black (*sumi*) and white and gold metallic scales on red (*hi*)

Variety	*Basic Description*
8. KOHAKU	White with red pattern
9. KOROMO	Robed. Black or blue over red (*hi*)
10. SHOWA SANSHOKU	Black base with red and white patterns.
11. TAISHO SANSHOKU	(*Sanke*) White base with red and black pattern

Trophies

Koi farm in Taiwan

Variety	*Basic Description*
12. TANCHO	Has a red (*hi*) marking only on the top of the head. The marking is usually round. Can be a *Tancho Sanke, Tancho Showa,* or a variety of other colors.
13. UTSURIMONO	Black base with only one other color in a checked pattern

DETAILED DESCRIPTIONS OF KOI VARIETIES

TANCHO SANKE

Hi Shusui

Shiro-Bekko

1. ASAGI & SHUSUI: Pale blue-black. Orange/red below the lateral line and orange/red lines on the pectoral fins.

A. Asagi: Scaled. Pale blue, with orange/red below the lateral line and pectoral fins.

B. Shusui: Doitsu Asagi: Large dark blue scales along the dorsal and lateral line. Blue back with orange/red below the lateral line and on the pectoral fins.

2. BEKKO: A white body with mottled tortoise shell patterns.

A. Shiro-Bekko: All-white body with black pattern on the back.

B. Aka-Bekko: All-red body with black pattern on the back.

C. Ki-Bekko: All-yellow body with black pattern on the back.

3. HIKARIMOYO-MONO: All metallic, except Ogon (#6), Showa (#10) and Utsuri (#13).

A. Hariwake: Orange or yellow pattern on platinum body.

B. Kikisui: Platinum Doitsu with yellow waves.

C. Kujaku: Red or gold on platinum with dark matsuba (pinecone).

D. Yamatonishiki: Metallic white, with red and black patterns.

Hariwake

Gin-Showa

4. HIKARI-UTSURIMONO: Metallic Utsuri (#13) and Showa (#10).

A. Kin-Ki-Utsuri: Black body with golden metallic yellow pattern.

B. Kin-Hi-Utsuri: Black body with golden metallic red pattern.

C. Gin-Shiro: Metallic silver body with black and red patterns.

D. Kin-Showa: White body with black and golden metallic red patterns.

E. Gin-Showa: Silver metallic body with black and red patterns.

5. KAWARIMONO: Unusual ones.

A. Aka-Matsuba: Dark red body with red pinecone (matsuba) reticulated scales.

B. Kage: Hazy gray pinecone shadows (usually on Showa and Utsuri).

C. Kanoko: Dappled red pattern, like a fawn.

D. Karasu: All-black body.

E. Hajiro: All-black body with white tips on the fins.

F. Hageshiro: All black with white pattern on the head.

G. Goshiki: Old style: white, red, black, dark blue and light blue. Modern style: white, red, black, dark blue and light blue with pinecone pattern on the back.

H. Kumonru: Black and white Doitsu.

Kawarimono

Matsuba

6. HIKARI MUJIMONO: One metallic color.

A. Ogon: Gold metallic scales, or yellow-gold metallic scales, or platinum scales. Can be completely orange.

B. Kin-Matsuba: Gold metallic scales with pinecone pattern.

C. Gin-Matsuba: Silver metallic scales with pinecone pattern.

7. KINGINRIN: Rows of metallic scales along the back over the pattern. Gold on red or yellow scales, or silver on white or black scales.

Ginrin Showa

Sandan Kohaku

8. KOHAKU: White body with red pattern.

*A. **Ippon:*** One straight continuous red pattern.

*B. **Nidan:*** Two separate patterns of red.

*C. **Sandan:*** Three separate patterns of red.

*D. **Yodan:*** Four separate patterns of red.

*E. **Godan:*** Five separate patterns of red.

*F. **Inazuma:*** Zigzag (lightning)-shaped single pattern.

*G. **Maruten:*** A round red spot on the head along with other red patterns along the body.

9. KOROMO: Robed.

A. Ai-Goromo: White body with dark blue pinecone on the red patterns.

B. Sumi-Goromo: White body with black pinecone on the red patterns.

C. Buдo-Goromo: White body with black scales on top of the red scales, creating a purple color in the patterns.

Sumi-Goromo

Showa

10. SHOWA (SANSHOKU): Old style: black body with red and white patterns, black on the head and black on the pectoral fin joints. Black rising from below the lateral line and about 20% white. Modern style: more white, less black, but with black still appearing on the head and pectoral fins.

Taisho Sanshoku (Sanke)

Tancho Kohaku

11. TAISHO SANSHOKU (SANKE): Tricolor Koi. White body with red and black. No black on the head, but may have some black on pectoral fin joints.

12. TANCHO: Red pattern on the head.

A. *Tancho Kohaku:* White body with single red pattern on the top of the head.

B. *Tancho Sanke:* White body, black patterns, with a single red pattern on the top of the head.

C. *Tancho Showa:* Black body, red and white patterns, with a single red pattern on the top of the head.

13. UTSURIMONO: Black body with only one other color in a large checkered pattern.

A. ***Hi-Utsuri:*** Black body with red patterns.

B. ***Shiro-Utsuri:*** Black body with white patterns.

C. ***Ki-Utsuri:*** Black body with yellow patterns.

Hi-Utsuri

CHAPTER TWENTY

KOI-RELATED JAPANESE WORDS

AKA BEKKO

A = ah, as in father, but shorter

O = oh, as in toe, but shorter

EI = a, as in day

E = eh, as in met

U = oo, as in loose or due

G = g, as in good

I = ee, as in teen

AI = i, as in mine

J = j, as in joy

Words of multiple syllables are pronounced without accenting a syllable.

KOI-RELATED JAPANESE WORDS AND THEIR DEFINITIONS

AI blue

AKA red/orange

AKA HAJIRO "red with white feathers on wing"

ASAGI "morning light," light blue

ATAMA head

ATAMA GA HAGERU or HAGEAGAR clearness of the head

ATO late *sumi*-appearing in adult Koi

BAI "plum"

BAKUI or KIBAKU system where water turbulence causes air to mix with and oxygenate the water

BEKKO turtle or tortoise shell

BENI orange base

BETA-GIN a form of scale considered the finest of the kinginrin scales, usually uneven over the body

BO stick

BOKE blurred sumi, more gray than black

BOTAN rose, peony

BOZU bald head

BU size

BUDO grape

BUNKA shiny pectoral fins (fry only; disappears)

CHA brown

CHIGYO unsorted fry

CHIKU bamboo

CHOMAN tumor of reproductive organs, mostly in females

CHUPA medium-quality Koi

DAGOI poor-quality Koi, culls

DAN step

DANGARA(DANMOYO) stepped patterns

DANMONO Koi with step pattern

DOITSU German (Deutsch)

ENAZUMA a lightning-like red pattern from the head to the beginning of the tail

FUCARIN between scales

FUJI SANKE metallic luster on the head like bubbles

GAKU deformed Koi

GIN silver

GIN KABUTO silver helmet

GINSUI silver water

GO five

GODAN five-step *hi*

GOROMO robed, blue-black or purple overlay

GOSHIKI five colors: white, black, red-blue, light blue

GOTEN ZAKURA "Palace Cherry Blossoms" pattern, looks like bunches of grapes

HACHI head (*atama*)

HACHIWARE the design made by a black line running diagonally across the head, important in *Showa* and *Utsuri*

HACHIZUMI the black pattern which runs diagonally across the head in a lightning design

HAJIRO white tips on the pectoral fins

HAKU white

HANA flowery

HANATSUKI A *hi* marking that reaches the mouth

HANAZUMI A black spot pattern around the nose and mouth

HARIWAKI yellow or orange on platinum "foil patches"

HEISEI Heisei era of Japan, 1989–

HI red, *aka*, fire

HIAGARI degree of intensity of the red color

HIBAN red area or red pattern

HIGOI rouge

HAJIRO "white feathers on wing"

HIKARI shiny or metallic

HIRE various fins

HOO AKA red gill plates

HOOKAZUKI red cheeks

HOSHI opening or window with a pattern

INAZUMA lightning

IKE the pond

IPPON MOYO solid *hi* from head to tail

IRO color

IRO NO SHIAGARI the finished or polished condition of the Koi, pertaining especially to color, texture and sheen

IROAGARI the degree of color intensity

IARISUMI gravel, like small black spots

ILSIGOKI "stone wall"

JIHADA texture of the Koi's skin

KABUTO helmet

KAGAMI mirror

KAGE shadow, phantom, or reflection

KAKU rectangular or square

KANA male Koi

KANOKO fawn-dappled

KARASU "crow"; black Koi, white or orange bellies

KASANE black that appears on the hi

KADO edge

KATA MOYO pattern on the side of the Koi

KAWA Doitsu variety, no scale (leather carp)

KAWARI non-metallic

KAWARIMONO all non-metallic Koi

KESUKI scales that are visible because of thin *hi*; also uneven color of the pattern

KI yellow

KIKUSUI "chrysanthemum water"

KIN gold

KIN KABUTO *"golden helmet"*

KINDAI modern or new

KIWA pattern edge, definition between markings

KOBOREHI scattered or slopped-over red

KOI carp/*goi*

KOBORESUMI scattered black

KOKE scale

KOKENAMI *Doitsu* scale alignment

KOMOYO small pattern

KONJO very dark, almost black

KONO KOHAKU *hi* markings, but solid *hi* on the head

KOROMO robed; also *Goromo*

KOZUMI small black spots

KUCHI mouth

KUCHIBENI red lips, or lipstick

KUJAKU peacock

KUMONRYU *"nine-spot dragon"*— black *Doitsu*

with white head and fins

LEATHER KOI Koi with no scales along the lateral line and only small scales near the dorsal line

MADOAKI scales with shadows under the skin

MAGOI wild carp (*Cyprinus Carpio*)

MAKIBARA *hi* that wraps around the body below the lateral line

MAKIGARI black pattern extends from the abdomen to upper area

MAKIKOMI the pattern extends from the upper area to the abdomen

MARUTEN circle (separate *hi* on the head) as well as body pattern

MATSUBA pine needle (Japanese) or pinecone (English)

MEN face

MENA female Koi

MENKABURI red head

MIDORI green

MIZU *"water,"* very light blue

MIZU HO *"rice spikes"* — German scaled orange *Ogon* with highly metallic black dorsal scales

112

MOMIJI "maple" or "autumn" colors: red, purple, and white

MONO class or group

MOTO original sumi (from fry to adult)

MOTOGURO black color at the base of the pectoral fins

MOYO "the pattern"

MOYOMONO one pattern (solid color)

MOYO NO KIRE sharpness of edge of color pattern

MUJI "nothing else" — solid color

MUJIMONO shiny one-metallic color

MUNABIRE the pectoral fin (see *Tebire*)

NARUMI light blue pattern (*Narumi Asagi*)

NEZU "mouse," "gray"

NI two

NIBANI secondary *hi* from color enhancer, poor quality

NIDAN two-step *hi*

NISHIKIGOI "brocade Koi"

NOSEZUMI the black pattern overlaps the red pattern

OBIRE the tail fin

ODOME (OJIME) the area between the last pattern and the tail fin.

OGON one-color Koi, also bold or metallic

OMOYO large, wavy, single pattern covering most of the dorsal

ORENJI orange

PLATENA white metallic, platinum

PONGOI good-quality Koi

RIN scales

SAKURA cherry blossom

SAN three

SANDAN three-step *hi*

SANKE three colors

SANSHOKU three colors

SARASA red spots on the back

SHASHIKOME scales covering the front edge of the pattern

SEBIRE dorsal fin

SHAGERU to finish, polish or perfect

SHIKAKU square or rectangular shape of head pattern

SHIRO MATSUBA white body with black pinecone pattern

SHIMEKAI to purposely stunt growth to preserve color intensity

SHIMI small black specks on *Kono Kohaku*

SHINZO heart (as in *Tancho* with heart-shaped crest)

SHIRO white

SHITSU quality

SHO pine

SHOWA era of Koi, 1926–1989; also variety of Koi

SHUSUI "autumn water," "autumn sky"; *Asagi* with *Doitsu* scalation

SUI water

SOKOZUMI faintly visible black, like a shadow

SUMI black

SUMI-NAGASHI black with scales outlined in white

SURE rub or scratch, external injury

TAIKE conformation of the body

TAISHO era of Koi, 1912–1926

TAMA-GIN pearl scale (also *Tsubu-Gin*)

TANCHO red spot on head, as on the Japanese crane

TATIGOI small Koi with potential to be of show quality. Much overused as a sales pitch

TEBIRE (MUNABIRE) the pectoral fin

TERI (TSUBU) (TSUYA) gloss, luster

TOBI cannibalistic fry

TOBIHI *hi* markings like splattered paint

TORA tiger

TOSAI in its first year

TSUBO *sumi* (black) on white skin

TSUBU GIN pearl scales

TSUBAKI camellia

TSUBOZUMI black spots on white area

TSUYA (see Teri)

UROKO scales

UTSURI reflection, changed

UTSURIMONO black base with one color in checker pattern

YAMABUKI yellow wild flower

YAMATO-NISHIKI Yamato's brocade – *Taisho Sanshoku* metallic

YAMIYO-NISHIKIA *Doitsu, Yamato-Nishiki*

YOGYO young fish, fish culture, fish farming

YODAN four-step *hi*

YON four

YOROI armor (*Yotsu*)

ZUIUN auspicious clouds, light purple

ZUNINABURI red forehead

Colors

HI red

SHIRO white

SUMI black

KI yellow

ORENJI orange

MIDORI green

AI blue

NEZU gray

CHA brown

ZUIUN light purple

BUDO purple

Metallic Colors

KIN gold

GIN silver

PLATINA platinum

REVIEW QUESTIONS

SHIRO UTSURI

Since we have covered so much information, we thought a review might be helpful. We have chosen a question-and-answer format, so read the question, tell yourself the answer, and then check the next chapter to see if you are correct. This will give you a chance to prove to yourself how much you have learned without feeling intimidated by a test. Once you have mastered the logic of Koi keeping, you will be able to differentiate between good information and bad and between good products and bad ones. You can be a successful Koi keeper.

1. How large can you expect your Koi to be at maturity?

2. How many years can you expect your Koi to live?

3. What is the single most important factor in successful Koi keeping?

4. How can you tell a Koi from a goldfish?

5. Does a Koi have a stomach?

6. Is a full-sun location the best choice for a Koi pond?

7. What is the coldest water temperature for feeding Koi?

8. Should your pond be in partial shade?

9. What do oxygenating plants do that can be dangerous to Koi?

10. How often should your pump circulate your pond water?

11. What pH high and low readings can Koi tolerate?

12. How often should you test your pond water for ammonia and nitrite levels?

13. In cold winter climates what are the necessary steps for overwintering Koi?

14. What are the possible reasons for fish rubbing (flashing)?

15. What piece of equipment is essential for the well-being of your Koi?

16. What is the name of the "good" bacteria?

17. What do the aerobic bacteria do that is so beneficial?

18. What is the easiest and safest way to rid your pond of algae?

19. Is the size of the UV sterilizer the most critical factor?

20. Why should the side walls of the pond be slanted outward 20°?

21. What device will keep the pollen and leaves off the surface of your pond?

22. What two ingredients are mandatory for an efficient bio-filter?

23. How much non-iodized salt is recommended per 100 gallons?

24. When is your new pond ready for the introduction of Koi?

25. What do you look for in a good Koi dealer?

26. What do you look for in Koi you are considering for purchase?

27. What is the procedure for introducing new Koi into your pond?

28. Are Koi and plants compatible?

29. What is the controlling factor for determining the frequency of feeding Koi?

30. When cleaning your pond, what do you do with your Koi?

31. How can you tell the difference between male and female Koi?

32. What happens to your pond when Koi spawn?

33. What are the best deterrents against disease and parasites?

34. What are the 13 Koi varieties?

35. What are the colors of a *kohaku?*

36. What is the Japanese word for pinecone?

37. Name the variety of Koi that has only a few large scales.

38. How many colors are on a *goshiki?* What are they?

39. Is the UV sterilizer installed before or after the bio-filter?

40. What is your favorite variety?

REVIEW
ANSWERS

HI SHOWA BRED IN TAIWAN

1. 20 to 22 inches (50 to 55cm).

2. With proper care, 50 to 70 years.

3. Water quality!

4. Koi have two pairs of barbels and goldfish have no barbels at all.

5. No.

6. No!

7. 50°F or 10°C.

8. Yes!

9. Remove oxygen from the water at night.

10. Your pump should be big enough to circulate pond water every two hours.

11. 6.8 to 8.2.

12. Test the water in a new pond every day; test a pond with an established bio-filter at least once a week.

13. By-pass the waterfall water back into the pond; unplug, clean, and store the UV; unplug and store the fountain(s); plug the skimmer(s); place a small pump with a PVC pipe extension on the outlet on a plant shelf to provide moving water and aeration so the surface of the pond does not freeze over. Remove any debris.

14. A change in pH or the presence of parasites.

15. A properly designed bio-filter.

16. Aerobic bacteria.

17. They convert ammonia and nitrite into nitrate.

18. By using a UV sterilizer.

19. No. The rate of the flow is the critical factor.

20. To avoid the pressure of ice on the sides of the pond.

21. A skimmer.

22. An even flow of water and oxygen.

23. One-half pound per 100 gallons.

24. When all the systems are running and you are sure there are no leaks, and when the water has been dechlorinated and the salt has been added.

25. Cleanliness in the dealer's pond or tank environment, knowledgeable explanations, and healthy, robust Koi.

26. Look for active Koi with clear eyes and clear skin, good conformation, and good, clean colors (and make sure that there are no sick Koi in the same tank or pond).

27. Float the bag, test the pH in the bag and pond,

remove water from the bag and replace an equal amount with pond water approximately every 15 minutes. When the pH and temperature in the bag are the same as in the pond, remove the Koi by hand and put it into the pond. Never pour the water from the bag into your pond.

28. Yes!

29. Water temperature.

30. Put them into a large, clean container filled with pond water; put the container in a shaded area, cover, and aerate, if possible.

31. Males are long and slender, females are more rounded and have "hips."

32. Ammonia levels spike, usually to dangerous levels.

33. Good water quality, good diet, and careful introduction of Koi, after making certain they are healthy and have been quarantined.

34. See Chapter 19.

35. White body with red (*hi*) pattern(s).

36. *Matsuba.*

37. *Doitsu.*

38. Five: white, red, black, blue, and light blue.

39. After!

40. This is your choice.

CONVERSION TABLES

KOHAKU

LINEAR MEASURE (LENGTH)

To convert	Multiply by	To convert	Multiply by
inches to millimeters	25.4	millimeters to inches	0.039
inches to centimeters	2.54	centimeters to inches	0.394
feet to meters	0.305	meters to feet	3.281
yards to meters	0.914	meters to yards	1.094

SQUARE MEASURE (AREA)

To convert	Multiply by	To convert	Multiply by
sq. inches to sq. centimeters	6.452	sq. centimeters to sq. inches	0.155
sq. feet to sq. meters	0.093	sq. meters to sq. feet	10.764
sq. yards to sq. meters	0.836	sq. meters to sq. yards	1.196

CUBIC MEASURE (VOLUME)

To convert	Multiply by	To convert	Multiply by
cu. inches to cu. centimeters	16.387	cu. centimeters to cu. inches	0.061
cu. feet to cu. meters	0.028	cu. meters to cu. feet	35.315
cu. yards to cu. meters	0.765	cu. meters to cu. yards	1.308

LIQUID MEASURE (CAPACITY)

To convert	Multiply by	To convert	Multiply by
fluid ounces to liters	0.03	liters to fluid ounces	33.814
quarts to liters	0.946	liters to quarts	1.057
gallons to liters	3.785	liters to gallons	0.264
Imperial gallons to liters	4.546	liters to Imperial gallons	0.220

WEIGHT (MASS)

To convert	Multiply by	To convert	Multiply by
ounces avoirdupois to grams	28.35	grams to ounces avoirdupois	0.035
pounds avoirdupois to kilograms	0.454	kilograms to pounds avoirdupois	2.205

TEMPERATURE

Fahrenheit thermometer		Celsius (or centigrade) thermometer
32°F	freezing point of water	0°C
212°F	boiling point of water	100°C

To find °C, subtract 32 from °F and divide by 1.8.
To find °F, multiply °C by 1.8 and add 32.

About the Authors

Nancy Cooper Wisner and Frederick Albert Simon operate Nishikigoi Garden Ponds, Inc., in Medford Lakes, N.J. They have dedicated the last five years to making Koi keeping a hobby everyone can enjoy. Their goal is to prove that it's possible to keep it simple and still be a very successful Koi keeper.